A Guide to College Success for Post-Traditional Students

D1300375

A Volume in:
Adult Learning in Professional, Organizational, and Community Settings

Series Editor:
Carrie Boden-McGill
Texas State University

Adult Learning in Professional, Organizational, and Community Settings

Series Editors:

Carrie Boden-McGill
Texas State University

Mentoring in Formal and Informal Contexts (2016)
Kathy Peno, Elaine M. Silva Mangiante, Rita A. Kenahan

Enhancing Writing Skills (2015)
Oluwakemi J. Elufiede, Carrie J. Boden McGill, Tina Murray

Building Sustainable Futures for Adult Learners (2014)
Jennifer K. Holtz, Stephen B. Springer, Carrie J. Boden McGill

A Guide to College Success for Post-Traditional Students

Edited by

Henry S. Merrill

INFORMATION AGE PUBLISHING, INC.
Charlotte, NC • www.infoagepub.com

Library of Congress Cataloging-in-Publication Data

The CIP data for this book can be found on the LIbrary of Congress website (loc.gov).

Paperback: 978-1-68123-917-0
Hardcover: 978-1-68123-918-7
eBook: 978-1-68123-919-4

Printed in the United States of America

CONTENTS

Foreword/Acknowledgements vii

Introduction ix

1. Designing a Project Plan for your Degree 1

2. Prior Learning Assessment 19

3. Useful Resources for All Courses 45

4. Official Course Descriptions for OWLS Courses Required
   for BAAS Degree 85

   Appendix A 95

   Appendix B 98

FOREWORD/ ACKNOWLEDGEMENTS

The purpose of this book is to assist students to achieve success in the Occupational, Workforce, and Leadership Studies (OWLS) Department and earn the BAAS Degree at Texas State University. The idea for this text emerged in a fall retreat workshop to revise the BAAS curriculum. Patricia Brewer, the workshop facilitator, asked the questions, "What do we want to build together?" and "What do students in the BAAS program need?" The following text offers the best thinking of the OWLS faculty and staff in regard to these questions. A two day workshop turned into a two year project, the addition of two new courses in the BAAS program (CTE 3313E Introduction to Interdisciplinary Studies for the Bachelor of Applied Arts and Sciences Degree and OCED 4111 Independent Study in Occupational Education), and significant revisions to all other required courses in the program (OCED 4350 Occupational Assessment and OCED 4360 Cooperative OCED Readiness, and 4361 capstone in Cooperative OCED).

The writing and publication of the book is part of a process of OWLS course and curriculum revision under the direction of Dr. Carrie Boden, Former Chair of the OWLS Department. Dr. Henry S. Merrill served as an external consultant assisting with the curriculum revision process and guiding the development of the book in collaboration with OWLS faculty colleagues Dr. Catherine A. Cherrstrom,

A Guide to College Success for Post-Traditional Students,
pages vii–viii.

Dr. Matthew Eichler, Dr. Patricia Gibson, Dr. Omar Lopez, Dr. Todd Sherron, and Ms. Barbara Wilson.

We also want to recognize and thank Portia Gottschall for her excellent proofreading and editing skills. Her attention to detail is an important contribution to make this a more useable book.

INTRODUCTION

WELCOME TO THE BACHELOR OF APPLIED ARTS AND SCIENCES (BAAS) PROGRAM!

Welcome to the Bachelor of Applied Arts and Sciences (BAAS) program in the Department of Occupational, Workforce, and Leadership Studies (OWLS) at Texas State University. The program is designed to serve adult learners like you (also called non-traditional or post-traditional students), who may meet some or all of the following criteria: 25 years old or older, attend school part time, work full-time, financially independent, have dependents, and/or did not receive a standard high school diploma.

For many post-traditional learners, completing a college degree is a lifelong dream that leads to upward economic mobility. According to the most recent U.S. Census bureau data, workers who earn a bachelor's degree earn 45.45% more than those who hold only a high school diploma (U.S. Census Bureau, 2015). In the OWLS Department, our mission includes helping you reach your earning and professional potential by providing a flexible, interdisciplinary plan of study in which you choose courses that meet your needs and interests. These hybrid and online courses feature active learning, experiential learning, critical reflection and self-reflection, as well as interaction with course content and peers in subjects

A Guide to College Success for Post-Traditional Students,
pages ix–xv.

ix

"Those professors are remarkable, they are second to none. They value your experiences that you've had out in the world, and not just in your first class, but throughout the classes. They're just as diverse as the student body."

- Sandra Brooks, BAAS, MSIS

FIGURE 1.   Sandra Brooks Testimonial.

relevant to career and other goals. Last, the BAAS degree includes an option to participate in prior learning assessment (PLA), a process that allows you to apply for credit for prior college-level learning in the workplace. According to alumni feedback and testimonials, the BAAS program has been transformational in the lives of students, as described in Figure 1 above.

Conceptually, the BAAS plan of study includes five major components: the foundational, cornerstone, occupational emphasis, professional development, and capstone modules (See Table 1). The foundational module is not so much a set of courses, but rather an introduction to the philosophy and practice of the degree, including individualized degree planning. The BAAS differs from other degree programs in that you, in consultation with an advisor, will create your own unique plan of study, including an applied capstone project. As an advocate and ally, this advisor will help you select the best set of courses to reach personal and professional goals. Next, in the cornerstone module, you will complete 48 semester hours, including the general education core curriculum as well as the Introduction to Interdisciplinary Studies for the BAAS Degree and Adult Development and Career Planning courses.

The program builds from this cornerstone to the occupational emphasis, professional development, and capstone modules. In the occupational emphasis module, you will complete 48 semester hours focused on past or current work experience and one optional course, Independent Study in Prior Learning Assessment, where you may complete a portfolio to apply for credit for college-level learning in the workplace. In the professional development model, you will select courses to build knowledge, skills, and abilities to meet personal and professional goals. As a key part of an interdisciplinary program of study, this module may contain one to three areas of emphasis totaling 21 semester credit hours. Finally, in the capstone module, you will apply what you have learned in an organizational setting. The capstone includes two courses in which you will design and complete

TABLE 1. Texas State University's Bachelor of Applied Arts and Sciences (BAAS) Program

Texas State University's Bachelor of Applied Arts and Sciences (BAAS) Program (120 SCH)		
Foundation What do you need to be successful in the BAAS program?		
Designed for you—an adult learner (also called non-traditional or post-traditional student)		
Accelerated, active, applied, experiential and, interactive learning. Critical reflection and self-reflection embedded in curriculum design		
Individualized degree plan and advising		
Cornerstone (48 SCH) Why are you here? What is the program about? What will you learn?		
General education core curriculum		
CTE	3313E	Introduction to Interdisciplinary Studies
OCED	4350	Adult Development and Career Planning
Occupational Emphasis Module (48 SCH) Where have you been?		
OCED	4111	Independent Study in Prior Learning Assessment (PLA)
Courses of your choice		
Professional Development Module (21 SCH) Where do you want to go? What knowledge, skills, and abilities to you need to get there?		
Courses of your choice		
Capstone Module (6 SCH) What learning can you demonstrate?		
OCED	4360	BAAS Capstone Part 1
OCED	4361	BAAS Capstone Part 2

an applied project related to your professional development module. The capstone projects are validated by on site-supervisors and experts.

The faculty and staff in the OWLS program are here to guide and support you on the journey toward completing your degree. We are glad you are here.

The Department of Occupational, Workforce, and Leadership Studies (OWLS) prepares students for workplace success. We accomplish this mission through an accelerated, applied, undergraduate degree-completion program and graduate programs, including working with students who seek a non-traditional approach in completing a degree. In addition, we value discovery and understanding and accomplish this mission through research and service. This is in keeping with Texas State University's mission as a public, student-centered, Emerging Research University dedicated to excellence in serving the educational needs of the diverse population of Texas and the world beyond.

OUR SHARED VALUES

In pursuing our mission, we, the faculty, staff, and students of Texas State University, are guided by a shared collection of values. Specifically, we value:

- An exceptional undergraduate experience as the heart of what we do;
- Graduate education as a means of intellectual growth and professional development;
- A diversity of people and ideas, a spirit of inclusiveness, a global perspective, and a sense of community as essential conditions for campus life;
- The cultivation of character and the modeling of honesty, integrity, compassion, fairness, respect, and ethical behavior, both in the classroom and beyond;
- Engaged teaching and learning based in dialogue, student involvement, and the free exchange of ideas;
- Research, scholarship, and creative activity as fundamental sources of new knowledge and as expressions of the human spirit;
- A commitment to public service as a resource for personal, educational, cultural, and economic development;
- Thoughtful reflection, collaboration, planning, and evaluation as essential for meeting the changing needs of those we serve (Texas State University, 2012).

PURPOSE OF THE BAAS DEGREE PROGRAM

You have begun an important journey—the journey to a bachelor's degree. As a student in the Bachelor of Applied Arts and Sciences (BAAS) degree program at Texas State University, you will be taking a number of courses to complete your degree. The degree program has only four required courses in common, unlike other degree programs at the university where a larger number of required courses would be part of the degree program. This text will act as a guide in those four classes as you move through your degree program.

Undoubtedly, as a student, you have questions about the degree path you have chosen. What will you do in your classes? What will you do in your degree program? What sort of a capstone experience will you plan to complete? How soon will you complete the degree? What courses will I take? How much credit will I receive in the prior learning assessment process? What will happen after the degree in terms of my career? What does this degree mean?

SEARCHING FOR ANSWERS

We all like definite answers and certainty about our decisions. Career, health, and financial decisions often consider what is certain, what is likely, and what amount of risk is present in any decision (Tversky & Kahneman, 1981). The BAAS degree program is unlike others at Texas State University and other universities.

Later sections of this text will reveal how these differences avail themselves to students in the program. For the purposes of this discussion, you should know that no two individuals in the program have the same plan to complete this degree. There are a variety of ways to complete the credits to earn your degree—and within each of the ways, there are a number of choices. The degree offers many options unavailable elsewhere at the university, however, with the variety of choices and unfolding of these choices, a high degree of ambiguity is part of the degree planning process.

One very tangible example of this ambiguity is the process of applying for credit for prior learning through the prior learning assessment (PLA) process. This process takes time as you develop a portfolio, for the portfolio to be checked by the instructor, assessed by evaluators, and for a credit recommendation to be developed and approved by the department chair. Since the number of credits received in this process can affect how many courses and what type of courses you take to complete the degree requirements, you may not know in advance what courses to complete until that PLA process is completed. The benefit of the PLA process in this case is that you may be able to receive quite a number of credits towards your degree, but the cost is that it takes time to develop documentation of your workplace and other learning, and you, as a student, will not know the number of credits to be received until after the assessment process is complete. This may affect how long the degree will take you to complete. This option for prior learning assessment is not available in other majors at the university and is of great benefit if you need the credits, but it takes time.

The search for answers, whether in your workplace, the university, or your personal life, can take time and patience. Indeed, Socrates wrote .".the unexamined life is not worth living," (as cited in Plato, 1966) holding high the virtue of reflection and the search for true knowledge. The tolerance for these ambiguities will assist you in working through your degree program and probably greatly benefit you in your future pursuits, whether they involve your career, your family, or your community engagement. Ambiguity in this context relates to what may be unfamiliar, incomplete, or overly complex, and the response you have to these situations. Some people respond with anxiety, while others are able to interpret ambiguous situations as situations needing further information or time before certainty may be reached. Another possible response to ambiguous situations is to be open to change over time, knowing that you may have to deal with limited information in planning or drawing conclusions, but that this may change over time as additional data are gained. While the tolerance (or intolerance) of ambiguity is seen as a personality characteristic (Budner, 1962), it does vary by the culture in which an individual was raised (Hofstede, 1984), and may be changed through thinking in new ways (Bartunek & Louis, 1988). We hope you will embrace this necessary ambiguity as you engage in your degree journey with us.

BRIEF DESCRIPTION OF THE CHAPTERS

This book is intended to serve as a guide for a degree with much flexibility, adaptability, and support for you as a learner concerned about your personal and professional growth. The purpose of the book is to provide information for you as a student throughout your time in the program. The book will serve as a text for core classes and as a handbook for degree completion. You will be introduced to a number of important concepts and be given a preview of your required courses as well ideas about how to design a project plan to complete your degree. You will be assigned to read various portions of the book for OCED required classes as you complete your degree. You may want to jump ahead and read sections to discover what will be coming up in the future courses. You will have many opportunities to make choices in your time completing this degree—we want to inform those choices as best we can.

Chapter One, *Designing a Project Plan for Your Degree*, presents an overview of the requirements to complete the BAAS in the context of project planning. This discussion invites you to view earning your degree as a project you need to design and complete during the next couple of years. Chapter Two, *Prior Learning Assessment*, provides background on prior learning assessment (PLA) concepts in post-secondary education and a guide to the process of developing a portfolio for the OECD 4111 Independent Study for PLA course. Chapter Three, *Useful Resources for All Courses*, is divided into six sections. These sections provide overviews written by faculty subject matter experts with resources for understanding effective writing processes; approaching research in your courses; becoming critical thinkers; creating a problem statement for your capstone; learning about project planning, human performance planning and career development; and, finally, increasing familiarity with the internet and computer technology. Chapter Four, *Official Course Descriptions for OWLS Courses Required for BAAS Degree*, provides the official course descriptions for CTE 3313E Introduction to Interdisciplinary Studies for the Bachelor of Applied Arts and Sciences Degree; OCED 4111 Independent Study in Occupational Education; OCED 4350 Occupational Assessment; and OCED 4360 Cooperative OCED Readiness and 4361 capstone in Cooperative. The final section of the book, titled *Appendix—Glossary of Terms for the BAAS Degree,* is a useful resource for understanding many of the terms and acronyms you'll hear at Texas State University.

REFERENCES

Bartunek, J. M., & Louis, M. R. (1988). The design of work environments to stretch manager's capacities for complex thinking. *HR: Human Resource Planning, 11*(1), 13–22.

Budner, S. (1962). Intolerance of ambiguity as a personality variable. *Journal of Personality, 30*(1), 29–50.

Hofstede, G. (1984). *Cultures' consequences.* Beverly Hills, CA: Sage.

Plato. (1966). Apology. In H. N. Fowler (Trans), *Plato in twelve volumes.* Cambridge, MA: Harvard University Press.

Texas State University. (2012). *Mission and goals.* Retrieved from http://www.txstate.edu/about/mission

Tversky, A., & Kahneman, D. (1981). The framing of decisions and the psychology of choice. *Science, 211*(4481), 453–458.

United States Census Bureau. (2015). *QuickFacts.* Retrieved from https://www.census.gov/quickfacts/table/PST045216/00

CHAPTER 1

DESIGNING A PROJECT PLAN FOR YOUR DEGREE

"If you're interested in something more than just the completion of a degree, you actually want to enhance your earning capacity or the entrepreneurial spirit that we have in this country, this is the kind of program that can help you build your specialty...the OWLS program really pushes that customization."

-Antoine Lane, BAAS, MSIS

FIGURE 1.1.   Antoine Lane Testimonial.

A Guide to College Success for Post-Traditional Students,
pages 1–18.

WHAT ARE YOUR EXPECTATIONS ABOUT COMPLETING A COLLEGE DEGREE?

The Bachelor of Applied Arts and Sciences (BAAS) degree is a degree designed to assist you in achieving a bachelor's degree through a variety of ways to earn course credits to complete your degree. In this section, we describe some of the ways to complete a college degree. This interdisciplinary degree program is customized based on your previous experience in education, the workplace, your current learning needs, and your future career and life goals, as described by the alumnus in Figure 1.1.

Many students complete a bachelor's degree by attending in the traditional pattern as full-time students immediately following high school graduation and mostly attending daytime classes. Online courses delivered via the Internet are another option with more courses available every year. At Texas State University, a majority of students follow this pattern. Many of the students in the traditional path at Texas State University study majors in which degree plans are very clearly described with required courses and a few electives. For example, if you were to pursue a degree in Mathematics, much of the required coursework is already 'spelled out,' and you might work with an advisor primarily to plan the sequence of your courses, selecting a minor (if appropriate), and reviewing your course performance.

There are, however, a significant number of students at Texas State who take evening or online classes or who have not been in school or university for some time. The BAAS degree is an excellent option for these post-traditional learners as well as for the more traditional learners. Your courses in the program will likely include students aged in the 20s through retirement age, as well as a mix of people from diverse walks of life. As we recall our students, we've had those with decades of experience in technical trades, technology work, public service, public service, military and many sectors of the business world. We have students whose primary work is in their home or in community organizations. We have some who have been very successful and already earn a high income. There are also those who are earning the degree to make a career transition. There are some students whose first language is not English and even those who come from other countries and continents as immigrants or refugees.

WHAT IS THE BAAS DEGREE PROGRAM?

It might be helpful to think about what this program is *not,* before moving on to some of the ways to think about the program. First, this program does not get you a Bachelor of Science or Bachelor of Arts (or any degree other than the Bachelor of Applied Arts and Sciences) in a major such as psychology, business, physics, mathematics, mass communication, English, or any other major other than applied arts and sciences. (We'll discuss some ways you can effectively describe what you accomplished with the BAAS degree in the next section.) The degree is not a degree that offers certification in any particular area, whether that's a teaching certification, certification as an interior designer, social worker, or nurse.

This degree program is interdisciplinary and personalized based on your previous experience in education and the workplace, your current learning needs, and your future career and life goals. The program, unlike others, offers a variety of ways to earn credits toward your graduation. These ways go beyond traditional daytime university face-to-face classes, and include online courses, hybrid (partially online) courses, evening courses, extension courses, correspondence courses, credit awarded for prior learning through the prior learning assessment (PLA) process, credits for military involvement, credits from testing programs like CLEP (College Level Examination Program) and DSST exams (known as DANTES for members of the military), credits from vocational/career courses at regionally accredited junior/community colleges, and transfer credits from other similarly accredited universities. The BAAS offers the most flexibility in accruing credit to meet your degree requirements; however, you will need to still take some academic "core" courses from Texas State University to receive the degree. Your academic advisor will fill you in on the specific requirements.

What is an interdisciplinary degree? These are degrees that focus on the development of broad generic skills applicable to a wide range of occupational opportunities. This is especially critical to employers when one considers that the average worker will probably hold six jobs requiring different skills in a lifetime. If your academic preparation is too specialized, it may not be applicable to some future jobs. Additionally, the knowledge explosion has caused specialized degrees to become dated. Therefore, interdisciplinary degrees emphasizing the development of skills that are not related to a single occupational path provide the greatest flexibility in career development. The broad liberal arts skills, such as effective communication and critical thinking, are what really matter once a person starts advancing in a career. Interdisciplinary programs are not for everyone. They are best suited for mature students who are motivated, able to learn independently, and have well-developed organizational skills.

What is an individualized degree? Traditional degree programs are prescriptive in nature and require that all students complete the same coursework, often available only in specific semesters. With an individualized degree, students determine when they will graduate and do not follow a set semester-by-semester sequence of required courses schedule. BAAS majors have the opportunity to select the courses for their professional development and identify a capstone project in OCED 4360/4361 based on personal life, work and career goals. Additionally, the credit hours in the occupational emphasis module can be completed in a variety of ways including applying for prior learning assessment (PLA).

Students sometimes inquire about the accreditation of the BAAS program. Texas State University degrees are accredited through the Southern Association for Colleges and Schools (which covers all of Texas within its region) as a university. Some programs at universities have program level accreditation, but many do not. Some examples of program level accreditations at Texas State include the Nursing Bachelor's program, which is accredited by Texas Board of Nursing and the Commission on Collegiate Nursing Education, and the Industrial Engineering Program which is accredited by the Accreditation Board for Engineering and Technology. (Please note that these accreditations were current at the time of writing this text; however, may be subject to change.) Program specific accreditations serve licensed/certified professions and those with rather specific career/professional outcomes. Most programs at Texas State (and many other universities) do not have these types of accreditations. This does not mean that the programs without individual program accreditation are "less than" other programs with programmatic accreditation. What it does mean is there is not a specific industry accreditation that applies to that program. In the United States, there are a variety of accrediting bodies that accredit entire universities or colleges to offer degree programs.

Most public (state) universities and colleges—including community colleges—are accredited through a review process with regional accreditation associations. Many of these regional accreditors also accredit other educational institutions than colleges and universities (such as secondary schools). In addition, these regional accreditors accredit private institutions (whether for-profit, non-profit, or tied to a religious denomination). Texas State University is accredited through the Southern Association for Colleges and Schools (SACS) as a research university. You can search for "regional accreditation" online for a full overview of this system. But please know that we can typically work with transfer credits from other universities and colleges that are regionally accredited, however we cannot work with credits from other accrediting agencies, including ones specific to certain seminaries and religious schools or career schools, which typically speak of "national accreditation." Accreditation is a complex issue in the United States. Being a university accredited by SACS allows Texas State University to receive public benefits such as federal financial aid programs for students. All the programs at a university accredited by a regional accreditor are considered accredited, including the BAAS program.

WHAT ARE THE MECHANICS OF THE BAAS DEGREE PROGRAM?

As you have read, the BAAS program is different from other traditional degree programs at the university. Instead of a long list of required courses to work through, you, in consultation with your academic advisor and instructors, will check to see how your experiential learning may work to fill a number of credit requirements for the degree, and develop a plan for completing the remaining credit requirements to earn your degree. Certain guidelines are in place for each of these areas in which credit is needed, and your advisor and instructors will assist you in understanding these guidelines. Because the degree program is part of a larger university, rigorous standards are present for completing the degree requirements.

Each student's case is unique and we value your work and life experience. We will do our best to help you complete the degree as quickly as possible given your situation.

The next few pages describe the rules for completing the requirements to earn the BAAS degree. Please do not despair—you and an academic advisor will design your project plan to graduation!

Where are Texas State courses available? When you are admitted to Texas State, it is possible to take courses for the BAAS in San Marcos, Round Rock, or online. It is possible to be a full-time student on the main campus. The Round Rock Campus (RRC) offers a limited number of junior and senior level courses with most of them scheduled in the evening. BAAS majors taking courses at the RRC generally work full-time and register for 6 credit hours. It is possible to receive financial aid if you are enrolled for a minimum of 6 credit hours, as that is considered being a part-time student.

What types of courses are available? Students have the opportunity to complete courses in a variety of different formats for the BAAS degree.

Live classroom courses. San Marcos is a traditional campus and most courses are held during the day (a limited number are scheduled in the evenings) with students and instructor together in the classroom.

Hybrid courses. These are online courses combined with in person classroom meetings. They usually have no more than three (3) scheduled meetings at a campus. The Distance Learning Fee is assessed and financial aid can be used for this type of course. The day and time the on campus class sessions meet is listed in the schedule.

Internet or online courses. These are totally online courses you will access from TRACS (the Texas State course management system) without any in person meetings. Note: there is a per hour distance learning fee for a 3 credit hour class. Financial aid loans normally pay for Internet courses. These courses are shown as ARR (Arranged) in the schedule. These are examples of the courses referred to by the alumna in Figure 1.2.

"I was able to do hybrid, and do one online per semester and an in person. So I think that the beauty of the program is being able to take one or two classes either online or in person to work with your personal schedule."

- Summer Salazar, MSIS

FIGURE 1.2.   Testimonial of Summer Salazar.

Correspondence Studies. Some departments offer courses through Correspondence. Undergraduate students may take up to 18 hours (6 courses) by Correspondence. However, if you are also taking courses by Extension (the most common is coursework for the Certified Public Manager certificate), then the maximum allowable hours for Correspondence will be reduced so the student does not go over the rule of 30 hours combined for Correspondence and Extension. Students may register for a Correspondence course at any time on their website and have up to 9 months to complete the course. Exams may be administered at remote locations. Financial aid loans do **not** normally pay for these courses. However, they do count as part of the 30 hours residency requirement. If a student is only enrolled in Correspondence Studies for a semester, it is necessary to reapply for admission to register for courses in CATSWEB. For more information see: www.correspondence.txstate.edu.

Extension Studies. Extension courses, such as those in the Certified Public Manager program are offered on-campus and at various off-campus locations. The times and locations for such courses depend on student need, faculty availability, and demand. If a student is only enrolled in Extension Studies for a semester, it is necessary to reapply for admission to register for courses in CATSWEB. For more information see: www.extension.txstate.edu

Certified Public Manager. For BAAS majors, the Certified Public Manager (CPM) certificate is available through Extension Studies at both the San Marcos and Round Rock campuses. To review information and begin the registration process, go to the website: www.txstate.edu/cpm and open the link "Application for Academic Course Credit at the Round Rock, San Marcos, and San Antonio Locations" and follow the instructions.

Additional Options for Completing Coursework. CLEP—College-Level Examination Program—www.clep.collegeboard.org. CLEP Exams are administered at over 1,800 institutions nationwide, and 2,900 colleges and universities award college credit to those who perform well on them. CLEP exams cover material directly related to specific undergraduate courses taught during a student's first two years in college. The BAAS allows unlimited CLEP Exams but they do not satisfy the 30 hour residency requirement.

Departmental Exams—www.txstate.edu/trec. The Testing, Research-Support, and Evaluation Center (TREC) administers departmental exams on an institutional basis only to currently enrolled Texas State students, former students, or students who have been accepted for admission for the following semester.

DSST Exams—http://getcollegecredit.com. DSST Exams were developed to enable schools to award credit to students for knowledge equivalent to that learned by students taking the course. The American Council on Education (ACE) recommends college credit for DSST exams.

Portfolio Assessment during OCED 4111 Independent Study Course. Students who plan to apply for prior learning assessment (PLA) through a portfolio evaluation process will register for this course following completion of CTE

3313E. OCED 4111 may be repeated to apply for credit in more than one area. Students should be aware that PLA does not transfer to other degrees and prescribed degrees may not use the assortment of courses in the Occupational Emphasis, recognize CLEP and DSST tests, Vocational Education (VE) courses, or military credit.

Texas State Degree Audit Report (DAR). You can access the Degree Audit from CATSWEB on the Texas State website. You can also do a 'what if' search on different majors to compare degrees. When you are initially admitted to Texas State, your DAR will only reflect core courses and all others will be listed in electives. After you attend a Degree Planning session, courses related to your work experience or a theme you designate will be moved from electives to the Occupational Emphasis (OE) module. This provides an estimate of how many hours are needed to complete the OE module and will help you decide whether to register for OCED 4111 to develop a portfolio, register for additional coursework, or complete coursework by testing with CLEP and DANTE. You will make the decision on how to individualize your DAR while enrolled in CTE 3313E, Introduction to Interdisciplinary Studies. It will be "finalized" following completion of OCED 4350 or OCED 4111 after the PLA credit award is added to your official Texas State course transcript. Once the DAR is finalized this is your contract with Texas State and you must complete the courses listed as your plan to complete the degree. If there are unexpected circumstances such as a department closing a course or it is not offered for several semesters, you may submit a petition to request a change in coursework.

About your GPA. When you transfer to Texas State, your former overall GPA is listed. After you have completed a course or semester at Texas State, there will be a Texas State GPA.

Enrollment catalog year. You have 6 years to finish the degree according to the requirements stated in the Texas State Catalog in the year you enrolled. Note: there is a difference in the number of hours needed in the Professional Development (PD) module depending on your catalog year. Beginning in Fall 2014 there are 21 hours required in PD module, of which 18 hours (five courses), must be related to the theme you have developed for your capstone project.

Modules and Degree Completion Rules. In order to graduate each <u>module</u> and <u>rule</u> must be satisfied. For example, some people may already have 120 college hours completed when they apply to Texas State but not all of the coursework will fit in respective modules for the BAAS. Having 120 credit hours completed on your transcript is just one requirement for graduation. The front screen of the DAR provides some information on rules. For example, it states 25% of the credits must be completed at Texas State which means 30 hours of residency. Residency requirements may be met by enrolling in online, blended, or face-to-face courses. Students should consult their advisor when planning these courses.

BAAS module structure. The BAAS is a modular degree program consisting of six modules:

1. General Education Core Curriculum (42 hours)
    Students enrolled at the junior/community college will follow the Transfer Planning Guide. General Education Core Curriculum courses may be completed in face-to-face courses at the San Marcos campus, or by CLEP, DANTES, Correspondence, and a small selection of online courses. Freshman and Sophomore-level core courses are not offered at the Round Rock Campus.
2. Occupational Emphasis Module (48 hours)
    This module relates to your prior or current career and/or college courses. It can be completed with academic and/or technical/vocational transfer coursework, credit from a military transcript evaluation, or prior learning assessment (PLA).
3. Professional Development Module (21 hours)
    Choose junior and/or senior level courses from three academic departments related to your future career goals. The Certified Public Manager (CPM) Certificate may be included in this module.
4. Foreign Language (8 hours)
    Students who have completed two years of the same foreign language in high school may be exempted from this requirement by submitting their official high school transcript at the time of admission. Students may also demonstrate this competency by taking sign language or satisfactory completion of a CLEP exam in a foreign language. Spanish may also be completed through Correspondence.
5. Electives Module (varies)
    The number of hours needed in electives is determined by what is still needed to satisfy the rules of degree completion. Do not take elective courses without consulting with your academic advisor.
6. Capstone Module (6 hours)
    This is the independent study project completed during the student's last semester while enrolled in OCED 4360/4361 courses (six credit hours total). Students on scholarships, financial aid, or veteran benefits should carefully plan courses to take with the capstone. The courses are complex and time-consuming, therefore, BAAS faculty strongly suggest completing the capstone without co-enrollment in other courses during the same semester. An alumnus describes the flexibility of the MSIS program in Figure 2.3.

Rules of degree completion. This section provides important numbers for requirements to complete the BAAS degree.

*   120—Total hours are required for degree completion
*   36—Advanced hours (3000/4000, ELADV) hours required
*   24/36—Advanced hours must be completed with Texas State
*   30—Hours residency must be completed with Texas State

- 15/21—Courses in Professional Development must be completed with Texas State
- 24 of last 30—Hours must be completed with Texas State
- 9—Writing Intensive Hours (WI) completed with OCED 4350, 4360, 4361
- 2.25 GPA—Required for professional development module
- 2.00 GPA—Required to graduate from Texas State

Other numbers important for BAAS degree completion. This section provides other important information about the requirements to complete the BAAS degree.

- 66—Junior/community college credit hours that can be transferred at time of application
- 2—Additional courses can be completed at the junior/community college level with permission
- 54—Texas State hours and a 3.4 Texas State GPA to be considered for Academic Honors
- 6—Years to complete the degree plan described in the catalog year you enrolled
- $50—Property Deposit on file that is refundable at graduation or can be donated
- 18—Credit hours that can be completed by Correspondence *(extension)
- 30—Credit hours that can be completed by a combination of Correspondence and Extension courses (like Certified Public Manager)
- No limit—University courses that can be transferred to Texas State
- No limit—Credit hours that can be awarded through CLEP and DSST

Academic advisors play an important role in helping you develop a plan to complete a degree as noted before all these rules. In the BAAS, you will make several important decisions about course choices and sequencing that will have some very real effects on the knowledge and skills you gain or when you might finish the degree. Since your BAAS degree project plan develops over time, it is important to stay in contact with your advisor and not try to self-advise. Self-advising is when students fail to utilize an advisor. In doing so, they may complete extra credit hours that do not apply toward a degree, enroll in courses in the wrong sequence, or even make unrealistic assumptions about their performance or ability to perform in a course or with a particular course load.

WHEN WILL I GRADUATE?

The BAAS is an accelerated degree with the time frame for completion determined by many factors unique to each student, such as:

- Number of credit hours transferred to Texas State University
- Number of credit hours awarded for prior learning assessment (PLA)

- Number of credit hours awarded for testing through CLEP and DSST
- Number of credit hours completed by Correspondence
- Number of credit hours completed by military transcript evaluation
- Number of credit hours completed each semester
- Number of credit hours completed during the summer

A graphic presentation in the form of a table to illustrate the project planning process steps along with the credit hour requirements to complete your BAAS degree is in Table 1.1. The far left-hand column is a list of the process steps you need to complete to earn the degree. In this example there are six columns that show a student entering in the Summer Term and plotting typical enrollment periods across two years.

TABLE 1.1.   Example of BAAS Project Planning Process Steps.

Planning Process Steps	Start – Summer Year 20xx	Fall Year 20xx	Spring Year 20yy	Summer Year 20yy	Fall Year 20yy	Spring Year 20zz
Complete Core – 42 credit hours (before applying for BAAS degree)						
Apply for admission to Texas State						
Required New Student Orientation (online option available)						
Complete CTE 3313E (1st 8 weeks)						
Complete OCED 4350 (2d 8 weeks)						
Include OCED 4311 (if necessary)						
Occupational Emphasis Module – Completed with transfer courses, PLA & testing (48 hours)						
Professional Development Module – (21 hours – choose Junior/Senior courses related to career goals)						
Elective courses – (as necessary to meet credit hour total)						

THINKING OF THE BAAS DEGREE AS A PROJECT MANAGEMENT EXPERIENCE

The Project Management Institute (PMI) is a major international training and development organization revolving around the concept of project management. You may want to look up their organization online if the idea of project management appeals to you professionally, as they offer useful information and professional certifications. Project management is one important conceptual focus available in the BAAS degree. It may be a useful metaphor for considering how to develop a plan for completing your degree program, as illustrated in Figure 1.1 (above). Before thinking about project management and your degree program, a definition is in order, which will guide your consideration in regards to your degree. According to Kerzner (2013),

A project can be considered any series of activities and tasks that:

- Have a specific objective to be completed within certain specifications
- Have delineated start and end dates
- Have funding limits (if applicable)
- Consume human and nonhuman resources (i.e., money, people, books, computers and other equipment)
- Are multifunctional (i.e. cut across several functional lines) (p. 3)

Obviously, project management assumes someone (or perhaps a team) manages the project. Completing your BAAS is a time when YOU are the project manager, along with your academic advisor as a strong partner in your planning process. Additionally, as a project manager, you need to consider to whom the project belongs. While first, you are the owner of the project, you also need to consider additional stakeholders and owners in the process. You are completing this project with the university, which is a state-funded institution, and the State of Texas is indeed a partner in your degree program. It is in the state's interest to develop qualified citizens as critical thinkers for a variety of purposes, namely to enhance democratic institutions within the state and produce a qualified and competitive workforce. Along with the state, you may have additional funders, such as the U. S. Federal Government through its grants and loans programs for higher education, a community scholarship program, agency, or even an individual paying for your education, or maybe your workplace through reimbursement for educational expenses. Your family may also be considered a partner in this project, depending on how this might affect them. Certainly, there may be economic effects beyond the cost of the degree, such as the opportunity cost of your time being involved in educational programs. There are also limitations of your time in contributing to family activities or maintaining a household during your time in the degree program. Further, family may be highly interested in the effects of increased income that might come as a result of completing your degree and advancing in your career. Your family and friends may be inspired by your degree progress (and ultimately by earning the degree) as well as being supportive when listening to your frustrations when you encounter seemingly insurmountable barriers to completing the degree according to the plan you designed.

WHAT IS YOUR SPECIFIC OBJECTIVE?

In this discussion, your objective is to receive your bachelor's degree at Texas State University. The particular specifications of the objective may refer to the degree program you are in, or the criteria under which you can receive the degree. For example, if your objective is to complete a degree in social work or agriculture or psychology or history, your project planning has already gone awry, because you are not in a bachelor's program that will get you a degree in these disciplines. You should also understand the rules presented above for completing requirements for the BAAS degree, such as how many credits you need, and in what areas, and with what grade point average (GPA), as described above.

WHAT ARE YOUR DEFINED START AND END DATES?

While the specific date of your graduation is not yet determined, the project (your degree) will have an end date when you have met the criteria for completion. This uncertainty was mentioned previously because of the number of options available for ways to earn the credits you may use towards graduation. When you receive the degree, the project is done, although that may be a good time to have another project, such as a graduate degree or career advancement activities, in mind. The project had a start date, either the date you started looking at completing your degree in this program, or some years ago when you started earning college credits towards a degree. However you view this—there *was* a start date.

As you come closer to the end of your degree completion, you can work with your advisor to predict your end date. You have chosen to complete your project at Texas State, and as such, there is a framework for which you can complete it. Just as you would not choose a builder for your house and tell them you need the house to be completed next week, you need to understand that projects do take some time to manage, to complete, and have multiple sorts of contingencies upon which the end date is dependent. Not meeting a goal for the closing of your degree may be disappointing, but it is not the end of the world, as you will probably have an opportunity to complete it later. This happens in projects all the time—they take longer than planned. One project management tool, the program evaluation and review technique (PERT), emphasizes the use of four sorts of estimates of time in project completion (Kerzner, 2013). While PERT uses statistics to deal with the likelihood of when a project will be completed, simplifying this can help understand how the time to completion may range.

Three estimates (*optimistic completion time, pessimistic completion time,* and *most likely completion time*) are utilized to estimate the *expected time of completion.* As you might have guessed, if your estimates are realistic, the time to complete the project will be somewhere between the optimistic and pessimistic completion times. Good estimates may be formed with your advisor; however, for most students, the BAAS will take at minimum three (3) semesters (Summer Term is also considered equal to a semester) to complete. Just as mentioned earlier, uncertainty is present in the management of any project. Unanticipated events arise that prevent the timely completion of the project. In some cases, the project may be caught up and in other cases, this delays the completion of the project.

WHAT ARE THE SOURCES AND LIMITS OF YOUR FUNDS?

If you are like many university students in the U. S., your degree is not self-funded with only your income. As an in-state resident within a state university, some funding for your education is provided by state and university mechanisms. These are rather indirect, and may not appear to affect you directly, but if you wish, take a moment to see what tuition would cost as an out-of-state student, without Texas residency, to get a taste for the actual cost of university education. The state has set limits on how many hours you may attempt at the in-state tuition rate. This is a funding limit—the state's interest is in seeing students efficiently move through a university system towards completing their degree. These limits are related to the number of times a course may be attempted and the total number of hours attempted. Exceeding these does not mean the university will stop you from enrolling, however, some of the cost will no longer be subsidized as much by the state.

You may rely on various scholarships, Federal programs (such as grants or loans or GI-Bill), or state programs for more direct funding of your program. Perhaps your employer is funding part or all of your tuition. In any case, the funding by third parties is likely to be limited. Many of us dip into our own personal savings, or maybe have loved ones who dip into their savings, to assist us with finances during education. We (as faculty at the university) know that high-quality education is not inexpensive—and so we want you to make the most of your time here. In any case, all of these sources of funding have limits.

In reality, the costs of attending university do go beyond course tuition and fees. Many courses require textbooks or specific supplies. You may have to purchase a computer and related equipment. You may have to invest in Internet access or find a space to study. There are costs related to transportation to classes if you are attending campus-based courses. Another item to consider is the opportunity cost of attending university. Opportunity cost refers to the lost ability to do something else with your time while occupied with another activity. In other words, while engaged in the actual time attending courses and studying, you are not able to engage in other pursuits, such as work at your employer, working with your family or household, or running a business during those hours. This does not mean you cannot do these things while enrolled—it just means it is highly unlikely that you can be performing work for your employer while writing your paper for class or attending class meetings. These opportunity costs may affect others, particularly your family—so be sure they understand your time obligations and continue to monitor how your enrollment in school may affect others. Be sure to remind them of this important characteristic of projects—they have an end date!

WHAT RESOURCES WILL BE CONSUMED?

Although funding is discussed above as a separate characteristic, money from your own sources is a major resource utilized in pursuing a degree. Further, time is a resource, whether your time spent studying, traveling to class, or getting the supplies, materials, and infrastructure you need to succeed. Resources such as pens, pencils, paper, and books are consumed in the process of participating in class. You probably need equipment, like access to a computer with the Internet and necessary software, which is a resource. You might even consider the means of transportation a resource, if you will be driving a car to class and utilizing fuel, accruing wear on your vehicle, and so on.

WHAT MAKES COLLEGE A MULTI-FUNCTIONAL PROJECT?

Generally speaking, in the project management and planning realm, projects are considered multi-functional because they involve people or resources that go across functional areas within an organization. This means they may involve groups such as information technology, human resources, marketing, and service delivery or some combination like this. Earlier, you read about the way in which there are multiple partners in your degree program, including those who work for the university, and loved ones like family and friends in your life. This is an example of one way multi-functionality is in your degree program. You might also think about the different ways completing a degree program will affect you. This goes beyond your academic/intellectual skills, but also ways it may affect your social life, your economic life (through increased career opportunities), your vocational life (thinking about how you'd like to spend your working and non-working time), and your professional life. In short, a degree like the BAAS can affect the way you think about the world, think about further developing your knowledge and skills, think about how others might attend university, and about the possibilities that exist in the family and career (and non-career) arenas of your life in the future.

HOW DO I THINK AS A PROJECT MANAGER TO COMPLETE THIS DEGREE?

Project managers have to consider multiple concepts when managing a project, like the questions listed below. One way to begin a project management plan for your degree would be to draft responses to each question.

- How long will this take (in whole and in parts)?
- What are the action steps to identify and complete along the way (as illustrated above in Figure 1.1)?

The BAAS degree has given me a huge advantage managing projects. By the time I finished my capstone I felt like I had been forecasting goals and breaking down tasks for years.

- Dan Reif, BAAS

FIGURE 1.3. Testimonial of Dan Reif.

- What resources will I use?
- What will I do if the project plan doesn't work in exactly the way I had planned? (How will I not let this derail my project completely?)
- Who will be involved?
- How will I organize my work/life around completion of the project?
- Who are the stakeholders to whom I should report and be responsible?
- What do I have control of? (And conversely, what do I not have control of?)
- What will happen at the end of the project?

Just as project managers in the business world think about what they can control and what they cannot, this is an important consideration with your degree. You cannot control university degree requirements, but you do have choices about how to meet them—and within reason, how quickly you will meet them. Just as you cannot expect a skyscraper to be built in two weeks, you know there is probably a minimum time to degree completion, but this can be extended to a much longer period of time if your progress is slowed. Unfortunately, individuals have little control over tuition and fees at a university, whether students, faculty, or advisors. We do know some ways to control excess charges (i.e. registering on time, utilizing exams to demonstrate learning for credit, utilizing PLA, taking some courses at a community college). However, there are still minimum requirements for completing the degree that are relatively fixed. Your advisor will assist you with information on many of these topics; however, as the project manager, you need to get resources in order, do critical planning, and carry out your project to a successful completion—graduation!

HOW DO I GET READY TO LEARN, CHANGE, AND GROW?

Change and growth are inevitable parts of the human experience. Life changes, whether considering your own self, your family, your social networks, your abilities at work and school, even the ways you think about purpose and meaning. Life unfolds before us and we can choose how we respond to this unfolding. Some may feel the need to resist change. Others may anticipate change and really want it, feeling a push for change in life. A positive way to respond to change is to focus and reflect on it and embrace both the path that has lead you to this point and the path you will carve ahead. There will always be this present moment, a past you cannot change, and a future with the potential for you to shape. Change is often stressful. We encourage you to think about ways to deal with stress that are healthy during your program—whether that's making time for fun, exercise, time with loved ones, or developing a new hobby.

One of the purposes of higher education is to enhance your ability to think critically in disciplined ways. Very few of us came to higher education with this set of skill already developed. We know you will be changed in many ways. Because of the nature of this degree, most students are with us for a relatively short period of time—and learning is accelerated during this time. We suspect you, like many others who have completed the BAAS, will look back on the experience as valuable to you, your career, and your thinking. You may at times, however, forget about keeping this end in mind as you are meeting course deadlines, or working to identify the necessary resources to complete your courses. Remember that many like you have completed the program, learned and grown as a result, and enjoyed success in family and community life as well as career development after completing the degree.

How do I stay motivated? As we have listened to our students over the years, we realize that there are various forms of motivation that individuals have for completing their degree. For some individuals these are related to the sorts of things you might expect after completing the BAAS:

1. Creating more opportunities for career choices
2. Advancing in your own present career
3. Improving your thinking, problem-solving, and project management abilities
4. Increasing your salary

Students who can keep these things in mind as they work through the degree requirements are likely to be big picture thinkers who are able to connect what might be a daily struggle or temporary barrier to overcoming the challenge and moving towards degree completion.

Other students have spoken about more intangible ways they are motivated. They know they are working on achieving something new and challenging, such as:

1. Being the first in their family to complete a degree.
2. Being able to show their family and friends how it is possible to succeed academically.
3. Knowing that they can achieve managing a project as big as a degree.

These ways are related to the personal satisfaction of achievement.

We also understand that some students complete the BAAS degree for reasons related to improving knowledge and understanding the perspectives of academic disciplines and improving their critical thinking, such as:

1. The ability to think in new ways.
2. The ability to learn a new language in their coursework.
3. The ability to increase knowledge and understanding of specific academic disciplines applicable to your current career path or support a transition to a different career path.
4. The ability to improve understanding of how people interact in the dynamic systems found in the workplace, community, and family.

Some people's motivation changes as they work through the degree. For example, one student conveyed that she was driven because of work advancement reasons, but then came to find the academic coursework in the degree stimulating, leading her to think about the world in new and different ways. We know your motivation for completing the degree may change as you change, and this is perfectly fine! We also know there is a strong social component to motivation in the degree program. You may think of your co-students or colleagues in the program as another circle of people or new network. You probably have circles of family, friends, and professional colleagues already, and adding another layer of colleagues in the BAAS degree program circle may not only connect you socially, but also professionally. It's not uncommon for students to share job openings, tips for finding employment within certain workplaces, and words of encouragement when difficulties are faced. On our OWLS Department's website, you will find videos and testimonials that reflect the motivation and thoughts of our alumni. Some echo these sentiments. You may have personal motivation to complete the degree that is reflected here, or it may be something totally different.

WHAT TYPE OF JOBS CAN I GET WITH THE BAAS DEGREE?

Many post-traditional students are currently employed and use the BAAS to advance in their current career. For people entering the workforce or wanting to change careers, many job postings state "bachelor's degree required" and since the BAAS is an accredited degree graduates meet that requirement. Some students use the BAAS to gain access to the next level of their educational or career goals including:

- Applying to a graduate program to complete a master's degree
- Applying to law school
- Applying to a teacher certification program

REFERENCE

Kerzner, H. R. (2013). *Project management: A systems approach to planning, scheduling, and controlling* (11th ed.). Hoboken, NJ: Wiley.

CHAPTER 2

PRIOR LEARNING ASSESSMENT

"From A to Z it's all about me. Everything in here is all just saying what is it that you want, what is it that you need to do, what is it you're looking for; never did I hear you know this is what other people do, this is how were handling this, this is how it's going to pan out for you."

- Rudy Gutierrez, BAAS, MSIS

FIGURE 2.1. Testimonial of Rudy Gutierrez.

A Guide to College Success for Post-Traditional Students,
pages 19–44.
Copyright © 2018 by Information Age Publishing
All rights of reproduction in any form reserved.

The information and processes for applying for prior learning assessment (PLA) in this chapter support the course OCED 4111 in the Bachelor of Applied Arts and Sciences (BAAS) degree program at Texas State University. The course provides students advanced theory and techniques related to the identification, documentation, and assessment of college-level work life and non-collegiate forms of learning. At the course conclusion, the student will have developed a competency portfolio documenting her/his prior learning to be considered as an instrument for awarding credit.

SECTION ONE—WHAT IS PRIOR
LEARNING ASSESSMENT (PLA)?

The practice of granting college credit for learning and knowledge gained outside the traditional academic setting goes back decades, with roots in the G.I. Bill after World War II. Prior learning assessment (PLA) began to emerge as a process of evaluating training for college level learning after WW II as veterans on the G.I. Bill earned college credits for military training. The OWLS program at Texas State was created in response to the Vietnam Veterans returning to Texas. Since then the program has adapted to include all post-traditional learners from the workforce and all occupations. We believe learners can demonstrate college-level knowledge and competencies based on knowledge gained from experiences outside postsecondary education.

PLA is a term used to describe assessment of experiential learning gained outside a traditional academic environment. Put another way, it's learning and knowledge that students acquire while living their lives: working, participating in employer training programs, serving in the military, studying independently, volunteering or doing community service, and studying subjects using open source courseware

Prior learning assessment documents college level knowledge gained outside of colleges or universities. Historically, prior learning assessment mostly occurred behind the scenes, partially because colleges avoided advertising that college-level learning can occur before a student ever interacts with faculty members. In the last 40 years, however, PLA has steadily grown as a valid method for assessing college level learning. PLA is breaking into the mainstream as private and online colleges have increased the competitive market to obtain a college degree.

A bachelor's degree is the educational standard for many careers in today's economy. As a result, emphasis on the need for a college education has also increased. Thus, the market of post-traditional learners/students is expanding and driving growth and innovation in degree completion programs. The Council for Adult and Experiential Learning and the American Council of Education are two PLA communities of practice that provide leadership and standards for the practice.

THERE ARE MULTIPLE APPROACHES TO PLA.

Prior Learning Assessment is not just one method or tool. PLA includes options such as:

- Portfolio-based Assessments—Assessment of student portfolios
- American Council on Education (ACE) Guides—Published credit recommendations for formal instructional programs offered by non-collegiate agencies, both civilian employers and the military
- Advanced Placement (AP) Exams—A series of tests developed by the College Board initially for Advanced Placement (AP) high school courses, including 34 exams in 19 subject areas
- College Level Examination Program (CLEP) Exams—Tests of college subjects offered by the College Board
- DSST Credit by Exam Program—Formerly known as the DANTES Program, owned and administered by Prometric, tests knowledge of both lower-level and upper-level college material through 38 exams
- Excelsior College Examination Program—Formerly Regents College Exams or ACT/PEP Exams, offered by Excelsior College, NY
- UExcel Credit by Exam Program—tests knowledge of lower-level college material; awarded Excelsior College credit can be transferred to other colleges and universities
- National College Credit Recommendation Service—(formerly known as National PONSI) evaluates learning experiences for non-collegiate organizations
- Evaluation of Local Training—Program evaluations done by individual colleges of non-collegiate instructional programs
- Challenge Exams—Local tests developed by a college to verify learning achievement

See more at http://www.cael.org/pla.htm#What Is Prior Learning Assessment (PLA)?

QUALITY STANDARDS FOR ASSESSING LEARNING

CAEL states " . . . assessment can be more than just a tool for measuring learning. It is also a tool that, when done well, can help the learning process. Students who are given good feedback during the assessment process can use that feedback to build on what they know and turn it into new knowledge as well as a deeper understanding of themselves as learners." (Younger & Marienau, 2017, p. viii).

The following Quality Standards for Assessing Learning are published by the Council for Adult and Experiential Learning (CAEL) in the Third Edition of *Assessing Learning* (Younger & Marienau, 2017).

1. Credit or competencies are awarded only for evidence of learning, not for experience or time spent.
2. Assessment is integral to learning because it leads to and enables future learning.
3. Assessment is based on criteria for outcomes that are clearly articulated and shared among constituencies.
4. The determination of credit awards and competency levels are made by appropriate subject matter and credentialing experts.
5. Assessment advances the broader purpose of access and equity for diverse individuals and groups to support their success.
6. Institutions proactively provide guidance and support for learners' full engagement in the assessment process.
7. Assessment policies and procedures are the result of inclusive deliberation and are shared with all constituencies.
8. Fees charged for assessment are based on the services performed in the process rather than the credit awarded.
9. All practitioners involved in the assessment process pursue and receive adequate training and continuing professional development for the functions they perform.
10. Assessment programs are regularly monitored, evaluated and revised to respond to institutional and learner needs. (Younger & Marienau, 2017, pp. 32–34).

HOW PLA CONTRIBUTES TO ACADEMIC SUCCESS

CAEL conducted a study on PLA post-traditional student outcomes. The study examined data on 62,475 adult students at 48 colleges and universities across the country. CAEL found that graduation rates are two and a half times higher for students with PLA credit. PLA students also had higher persistence rates and a faster time to degree completion. For more information go to: http://www.cael.org/what-we-do/prior-learning-assessment#sthash.7GkfkAJd.dpuf

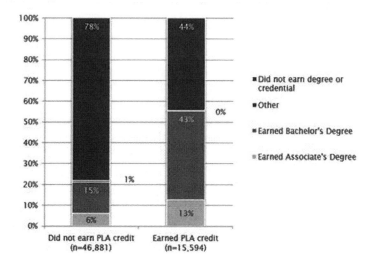

FIGURE 2.2.   CAEL Degree Completion by PLA Credit.

SECTION TWO—DEVELOPING A COMPETENCY PORTFOLIO

In this section you will see how to create your competency portfolio. Your competency portfolio is the manuscript that documents your skills, knowledge/cognitive processes, and tools and technology acquired from working and/or training. Each portfolio is assessed for college-level learning by two independent assessors. The two assessors' ratings are averaged and correlated with the academic credit recommendations.

First, students must develop a work life competency portfolio based on a previous or current occupation. Students can repeat OCED 4111 if more credit is needed to complete the Occupational Emphasis (OE) requirements for your degree. See the Policies and Procedures. A student may develop an additional work life portfolio assuming they did not reach the maximum of the 24 hour work life credit award. Each PLA vehicle, work life and non-collegiate learning, is limited to 24 hours and 30 hours, respectfully. Some students who have multiple hours of professional trainings or certifications can develop an additional competency portfolio for non-collegiate training. The training must relate to your previous work life portfolio and/or Occupational Emphasis in your degree plan.

Page One of Competency Portfolio

The first page of your competency portfolio is the application; it should be typed and notarized. See Table 2.1 Application for Work Life Learning and Table 2.2 Application for Non-collegiate Sponsored Instruction below for examples.

TABLE 2.1.   Application for Work Life Learning.

Application for Work Life Learning

O*NET.#_____

| Applicant's Name_____ | ID_____ | GPA_____ | DATE_____ |

Address_____   Home Phone_____   Work Phone_____

Work Experience

Date From – To	Years/ Months Exp	Employer	Location	Job Title and Rank or Grade	Name, Address, and Phone Number of Individual Who can Verify and Evaluate Experience

I, the undersigned, do solemnly affirm that the information furnished on this application is accurate and waive my right to appeal the evaluation of work life experience.

Signature_____

Subscribed and sworn to before me this _____ day of _____ 20 _____.

_____   _____   _____
Notary Public   County   State

TABLE 2.2.   Application for Non-sponsored Collegiate Instruction.

Application for Non-collegiate Sponsored Instruction

Applicant's Name_____   ID_____   Date_____

Address_____   Home Phone_____   Work Phone_____

Non-collegiate Sponsored Instruction

Dates	Course Title	Where Completed	Contact Hours	A.C.E. Number	A.C.E. Page Number

I, the undersigned, do solemnly affirm that the information furnished on this application is accurate and true.
Signature

_____

Subscribed and sworn to before me this _____ day of _____ 20 _____.

_____   _____   _____
Notary Public   County   State

Page Two of Competency Portfolio

The second page of your competency portfolio is a position description for the occupation or training that you are applying for academic credit.

Position description. The Position Description includes the following information.

Applicant's Name:

Employer:

Employer's address:

Job Title:

O*Net #:

General Job Description:

Examples of Work Performed (Situation, Action, & Result):

Experience and Training Requirements:

Educational Requirements:

Page Three of Competency Portfolio

The third page of the competency portfolio is the Job Task Analysis (JTA).

After searching the O*NET to identify your O*Net occupation number and title, study the tasks, skills, knowledge in the occupational profile to assist you in identifying the skills that you have developed in your occupation. Some of the tasks and skills listed in the O*NET may not be applicable to your skill set. The O*NET is only meant to serve as a guide for your JTA development. Through job task analysis, we can identify the macro, mid-level and micro skills that you used on a specific job. Remember we are only interested in those skills that are equivalent to college level learning. The JTA also organizes macro and micro skill clusters/ categories. Each skill/task is mutually exclusive; that is, they are unique and different skills.

The task analysis process identifies and sequences three level of skills:

Step 1: Identify and sequence three—five macro categories of level 1 instrumental skills.

Step 2: Analyze and divide each Level One instrumental skill into sub-skills that are named Level Two component skills. There should be two—three component skills for each instrumental skill.

Step 3:   Analyze and divide each Level Two component skill into Level Three atomistic skills. There should be at least two atomistic skills per each component skill.

Essentially, you will develop a skills map, macro to micro skills, you perform for your job. Your JTA will drive the development of your competency statements. You will write 25 competency statements that correlate to each Level 3 Atomistic Skill on your task analysis. See Figure 2.3 (below), for an example of a

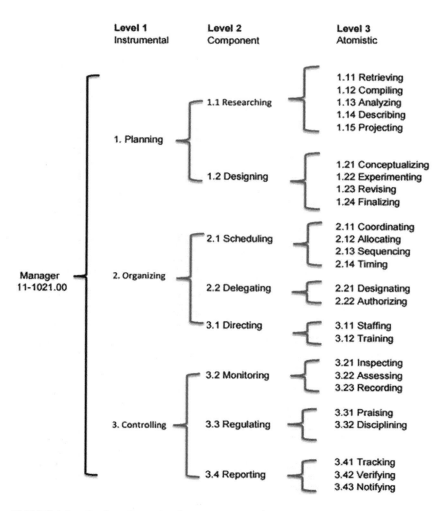

FIGURE 2.3.   Student Example of a Manager JTA from OCED 4111.

JTA for a manger position and Figure 2.4 for an example of a JTA for an administrative assistant position.

All Level Three Atomistic Skills on your JTA must meet the following criteria to be evaluated for academic credit:

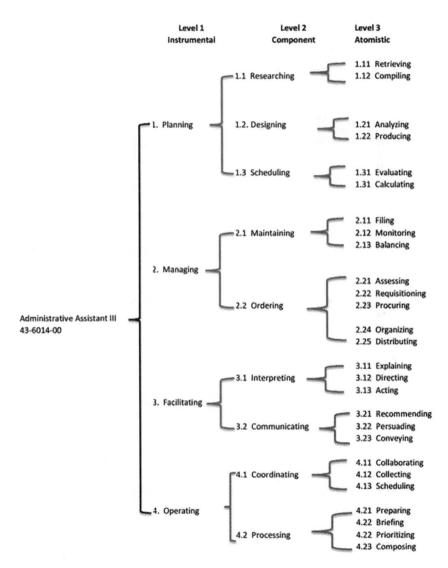

FIGURE 2.4.   Student Example of an Administrative Assistant JTA from OCED 4111.

1. Must be observable and verifiable.
2. Must be measureable. Quantitative and qualitative performance characteristics
3. Must be related to your Occupational Emphasis
4. Must be at a college level learning competency

Page Four of Competency Portfolio—Developing Competency Statements

If you are applying for Work Life learning credit you must develop 25 competency statements. If you are applying for Non-collegiate training credits you must develop 32 Competency statements. Each competency statement should be 1—2 pages maximum. Work life portfolios require a minimum of 8 competency statements up to 25 competency statements for a potential 24 hour credit award; and a non-collegiate portfolio requires a minimum of 8 competency statements up to 32 competency statements for a potential 30 hour competency award. .

A. The competency statement is structured this way.
- **Level One skill**: Insert your Level One skill here:

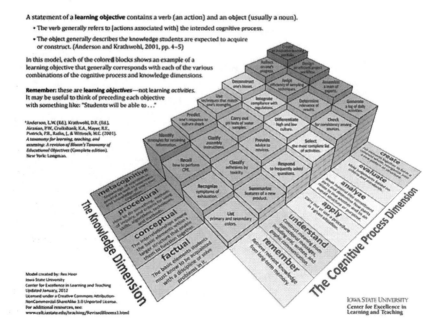

FIGURE 2.5. Knowledge and Cognitive Dimensions of Learning Objectives. Reproduced from Heer, 2012.

- **Level Two skill**: Insert your Level Two skill here:
- **Level 3: I can** (insert your Level Three skill here and quantitative characteristic here); <u>well enough to</u> (Insert qualitative characteristic here).

B. **The Knowledge and Cognitive Dimensions**. The Knowledge and Cognitive Dimensions contain four types of knowledge and five levels of cognitive processing dimensions. Use these types of knowledge and cognitive dimensions to describe your knowledge and cognitive skills used to execute the skill listed in your skill statement. See Figure 2.5 to see a graphic presentation of the interaction of the Knowledge and Cognitive dimensions.

- ***Knowledge dimension.*** You begin analysis of the Knowledge Dimension by asking yourself If I have knowledge of _____? What knowledge do I need to know in order to document and complete the skill listed in my competency statements? You may or may not be able to speak to all levels for each competency statement.

If I have,

- ***Factual Knowledge.*** Relevant terminology, knowledge of specific details and elements
- ***Conceptual knowledge***. Classifications and categories; and knowledge of principles and generalizations; knowledge of theories, models and structures
- ***Procedural Knowledge.*** Subject-specific skills and algorithms; knowledge of subject-specific techniques and methods; knowledge of criteria for determining when to use appropriate procedure
- ***Metacognitive: Strategic Knowledge.*** Knowledge about cognitive tasks including appropriate contextual and conditional knowledge self-knowledge
- **Cognitive dimension.** You begin analysis of the Cognitive Dimension by asking yourself for this skill, which of these cognitive dimensions do I use: understand, apply, analyze, evaluate, and/or create (Anderson & Krathwohl, 2001)? What cognitive processes do you need to perform in order to complete the skill listed in you competency statements? You may or may not be able to speak to all levels.

If I,

- ***Understand:*** Demonstrate understanding of facts and ideas by organizing, comparing, translating, interpreting, giving descriptions, and stating main ideas.
- ***Apply:*** Solve problems to new situations by applying acquired knowledge, facts, techniques and rules in a different way.

- *Analyze:* Examine and break information into parts by identifying motives or causes. Make inferences and find evidence to support generalizations.
- *Evaluate:* Present and defend opinions by making judgments about information, validity of ideas, or quality of work based on a set of criteria.
- *Create:* Compile information together in a different way by combining elements in a new pattern or proposing alternative solutions.

C. **Tools and technology.** What are the physical conditions (e.g. In a professional office setting with a desk, chair, computer, printer, and internet)? List, describe, and explain what tools and technology are needed to perform the skill in Section A above.
If I have, or If I use. . .

The total length of the portfolio will be longer than four pages after you have completed each of these sections described above: the application(s) for life work learning and/or non-collegiate sponsored instruction; position description; job task analysis; and multiple competency statements. The instructor of OCED 4111 will help guide you through this process.

SECTION THREE—HOW ARE COMPETENCY STATEMENTS DEVELOPED AND ASSESSED

A competency statement encompasses a skill statement, knowledge/cognitive process descriptions, & tools and technology statement. This section provides an expanded discussion of developing competency statements and outlines how the completed portfolio is assessed.

A. **Skills statement.** A skill statement defines your skill level in terms of quantitative and qualitative performance characteristics. Use your Level Three Atomistic Skills from your JTA to write your skill statements.

I can (insert your Level Three skill and quantitative characteristic here); Well enough to (Include performance criteria that are quantitative and qualitative in a nature). For example, " I can conduct 20 sales events, demonstrations, and national trade shows; Well enough to implement successfully at over 100 regional locations, 20 departments, and 4 national conferences on time, within budget, and without logistical issues." If both characteristics are present = 100 points; If only one characteristic is present = 50 points; If none are present = 0

B. **Knowledge dimension.** The knowledge dimension is your analysis of the levels of knowledge (factual, conceptual, procedural, and metacognitive) you can identify to document the skill identified in your competency statement. You may or may not be able to speak to all levels in each competency statement.

If I have:
- **Factual:** Knowledge of terminology; knowledge of specific details and elements
- **Conceptual**: Knowledge of classifications and categories; and Knowledge of principles and generalizations; Knowledge of theories, models and structures
- **Procedural:** Knowledge of subject-specific skills and algorithms; Knowledge of subject-specific techniques and methods; Knowledge of criteria for determining when to use appropriate procedure

- **Metacognitive:** Strategic Knowledge; Knowledge about cognitive tasks including appropriate contextual and conditional knowledge self-knowledge.

C. **Cognitive dimension.** The Cognitive Dimension represents a continuum of increasing cognitive complexity—from lower order thinking skills to higher order thinking skills. Five levels of cognitive processing dimensions are applicable here. The lowest order category, Remembering: Recognizing identifying, recalling, retrieving, is not considered college level learning and scores zero points. Higher cognitive dimensions yield higher scores and should be discussed at length in your competency statement.

If I

- *Understand.* Demonstrate understanding of facts and ideas by organizing, comparing, translating, interpreting, giving descriptions, and stating main ideas.
- *Apply.* Solve problems to new situations by applying acquired knowledge, facts, techniques and rules in a different way.
- *Analyze.* Examine and break information into parts by identifying motives or causes. Make inferences and find evidence to support generalizations.
- *Evaluate.* Present and defend opinions by making judgements about information, validity of ideas, or quality of work based on a set of criteria.

lower order thinking skills ———————————————————————————→ higher order thinking skills					
remember	**understand**	**apply**	**analyze**	**evaluate**	**create**
recognizing • identifying recalling • retrieving	interpreting • clarifying • paraphrasing • representing • translating exemplifying • illustrating • instantiating classifying • categorizing • subsuming summarizing • abstracting • generalizing inferring • concluding • extrapolating • interpolating • predicting comparing • contrasting • mapping • matching explaining • constructing models	executing • carrying out implementing • using	differentiating • discriminating • distinguishing • focusing • selecting organizing • finding coherence • integrating • outlining • parsing • structuring attributing • deconstructing	checking • coordinating • detecting • monitoring • testing critiquing • judging	generating • hypothesizing planning • designing producing • constructing

FIGURE 2.6. Categories and Cognitive Processes With Additional Descriptors. "Adapted from Anderson and Krathwohl, 2001, pp. 67–68. Reproduced from Heer, 2012.

- ***Create.*** Compile information together in a different way by combining elements in a new pattern or proposing alternative solutions.

The expanded description below of each of these Cognitive Dimensions provides additional terms that may be helpful in developing your JTA. The range of points awarded for each dimension is listed at the end of each description.

- ***Understand.*** Demonstrate understanding of facts and ideas by organizing, comparing, translating, interpreting, giving descriptions, and stating main ideas. Exemplifying, illustrating; classifying, categorizing, subsuming; summarizing, abstracting, generalizing; inferring, concluding, extrapolating, interpolating, predicting; comparing, contrasting, mapping, matching; explaining, constructing models" *equals 50–59 points.*
- ***Apply.*** Solve problems to new situations by applying acquired knowledge, facts, techniques and rules in a different way. Executing, carrying out, implementing, using *equals 60–69 points.*
- ***Analyze.*** Examine and break information into parts by identifying motives or causes. Make inferences and find evidence to support generalizations. "Differentiating, discriminating, distinguishing, focusing, selecting. Organizing, finding Coherence, integrating, outlining, parsing, structuring Attributing, deconstructing" *equals 70–79 points.*
- ***Evaluate.*** Present and defend opinions by making judgments about information, validity of ideas, or quality of work based on a set of criteria. "Checking, coordinating, detecting, monitoring. Testing; Critiquing, judging" *equals 80–89 points.*
- ***Create.*** Compile information together in a different way by combining elements in a new pattern or proposing alternative solutions." Generating, hypothesizing; Planning, designing; Producing, constructing" *equals 90–100 points.*

D. **Tools and technology.** What are the physical conditions (e.g. In a professional office setting with a desk, chair, computer, printer, and internet)? List, describe, and explain what tools and technology are needed to perform the skill in Section A above.

Answer the question If I have, or If I use. . . ? The overall use of tools and technology needed to perform skill is assessed from 0 to 100; where, 0 is no use and 100 is exceptional use. This section also includes a description of the physical conditions.

OWLS PLA COMPETENCY MODEL

The OWLS department has championed PLA practices for more than 40 years. Dr. Todd Sherron, developed the current competency model by integrating Bloom's

TABLE 2.3. Work Life Learning Performance Indicator Score.

Lowest Score		Highest Score	
Total Competency Factor	0	Total Competency Factor	10000
Portfolio Score	70	Portfolio Score	100
O*NET Job Zone (1-5) × 15	15	O*NET Job Zone (1-5) × 15	75
Specific Vocational Preparation (1-9) × 3	3	Specific Vocational Preparation (1-9) × 3	27
Performance Indicator Score	88	Performance Indicator Score	10200

revised taxonomy and components from Texas State's historical PLA model, "Discovering your Hidden Degree" (Pierson, 2002). Competency statements, encompassing a skill statement, knowledge/cognitive process descriptions, and tools and technology statements, are the foundation of the PLA portfolio. O*NET Job Zone and Specific Vocational Preparation (SVP) measures are used in the competency model calculation, as described below. The PLA Competency Model is described in detail below in Figure 2.7.

Work life learning performance indicator score. The Workforce Learning Performance Indicator is a score derived from the Total Competency Factor, Portfolio, Job Zone, and Specific Vocational Preparation scores. The Performance Indicator score ranges from 88 to 10200 and correlates to the number of credit hours awarded (ranges from 3 to 24 credit hours); that is, for each 3-hour increase in credit awarded there is 1300 point increase in the performance indicator score. The Portfolio Score is the instructor of record evaluated score, Job Zone (1–5) ×15 (a multiply was used to enlarge the variance in the measurement model)

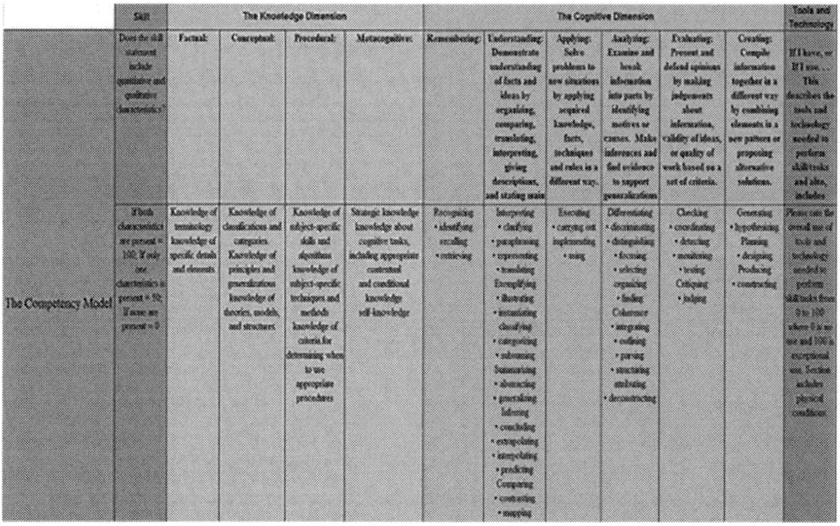

FIGURE 2.7.   PLA Competency Model © 2017 by Dr. Todd Sherron.

TABLE 2.4. Work Life Learning Performance Indicator Score with Credit Awards.

Performance Indicator Score	88-1300	1301-2600	2601-3900	3901-5200	5201-6500	6501-7800	7801-9100	9101-10400
Number of Hours Awarded	3	6	9	12	15	18	21	24

TABLE 2.5. Non-collegiate Learning Performance Indicator Score.

Lowest Score		**Highest Score**	
Total Competency Factor	0	Total Competency Factor	12800
Portfolio Score	70	Portfolio Score	100
O*NET Job Zone (1-5) × 15	15	O*NET Job Zone (1-5) × 5	75
Specific Vocational Preparation (1-9) × 3	3	Specific Vocational Preparation (1-9) × 3	27
Performance Indicator Score	88	Performance Indicator Score	13000

TABLE 2.6. Non-Collegiate Learning Performance Indicator Score with Credit Awards

Performance Indicator Score	88-1300	1301-2600	2601-3900	3901-5200	5201-6500	6501-7800	7801-9100	9101-10400	10401-11700	11701-13000
Number of Hours Awarded	3	6	9	12	15	18	21	24	27	30

and Specific Vocational Preparation $(1-9) \times 3$ (a multiply was used to enlarge the variance in the measurement model) are measures provided by the O*NET.

Non-collegiate learning performance indicator score. The Non-collegiate Performance Indicator is an average score derived from the Total Competency Factor, Portfolio, Job Zone, and Specific Vocational Preparation scores. The Performance Indicator score ranges from 88 to 13,000 and correlates to the number of hours awarded (3 hrs. to 30 hrs.); that is, for each 3 hour increase in credit awarded there is 1300 point increase in the performance indicator score. The Portfolio Score is the instructor of record evaluated score, Job Zone $(1–5) \times 15$ (a multiply was used to enlarge the variance in the measurement model) and Specific Vocational Preparation $(1–9) \times 3$ (a multiply was used to enlarge the variance in the measurement model) are measures provided by the O*NET.

*O*NET Measures.* O*NET Job Zone and Specific Vocational Preparation (SVP) measures are used in the competency model calculation.

Job Zones. The source of this section is O*Net: https://www.onetonline.org/help/online/zones A Job Zone is a group of occupations that are similar in:

- How much education people need to do the work.
- How much related experience people need to do the work.

- How much on-the-job training people need to do the work.

The five Job Zones are:

- Job Zone 1—occupations that need little or no preparation
- Job Zone 2—occupations that need some preparation
- Job Zone 3—occupations that need medium preparation
- Job Zone 4—occupations that need considerable preparation
- Job Zone 5—occupations that need extensive preparation

The five Job Zones with Specific Vocational Preparation are described with more detail in Table 2.7.

Specific Vocational Preparation (SVP). The source of this section is O*Net: https://www.onetonline.org/help/online/svp Specific Vocational Preparation is a

TABLE 2.7.   Job Zones for Specific Vocational Preparation.

Job Zone One: Little or no preparation needed	
Education	Some of these occupations may require a high school diploma or GED certificate.
Related Experience	Little or no previous work-related skill, knowledge, or experience is needed for these occupations. For example, a person can become a waiter or waitress even if he/she has never worked before.
Job Training	Employees in these occupations need anywhere from a few days to a few months of training. Usually, an experienced worker could show you how to do the job.
Job Zone Examples	These occupations involve following instructions and helping others. Examples include taxi drivers, amusement and recreation attendants, counter and rental clerks, nonfarm animal caretakers, continuous mining machine operators, and waiters/waitresses.
SVP Range	(Below 4.0)
Job Zone Two: Some preparation needed	
Education	These occupations usually require a high school diploma.
Related Experience	Some previous work-related skill, knowledge, or experience is usually needed. For example, a teller would benefit from experience working directly with the public.
Job Training	Employees in these occupations need anywhere from a few months to one year of working with experienced employees. A recognized apprenticeship program may be associated with these occupations.
Job Zone Examples	These occupations often involve using your knowledge and skills to help others. Examples include sheet metal workers, forest fire fighters, customer service representatives, physical therapist aides, salespersons (retail), and tellers.
SVP Range	(4.0 to < 6.0)

TABLE 2.7. Continued.

	Job Zone Three: Medium preparation needed
Education	Most occupations in this zone require training in vocational schools, related on-the-job experience, or an associate's degree.
Related Experience	Previous work-related skill, knowledge, or experience is required for these occupations. For example, an electrician must have completed three or four years of apprenticeship or several years of vocational training, and often must have passed a licensing exam, in order to perform the job.
Job Training	Employees in these occupations usually need one or two years of training involving both on-the-job experience and informal training with experienced workers. A recognized apprenticeship program may be associated with these occupations.
Job Zone Examples	These occupations usually involve using communication and organizational skills to coordinate, supervise, manage, or train others to accomplish goals. Examples include food service managers, electricians, agricultural technicians, legal secretaries, occupational therapy assistants, and medical assistants.
SVP Range	(6.0 to < 7.0)
	Job Zone Four: Considerable preparation needed
Education	Most of these occupations require a four-year bachelor's degree, but some do not.
Related Experience	A considerable amount of work-related skill, knowledge, or experience is needed for these occupations. For example, an accountant must complete four years of college and work for several years in accounting to be considered qualified.
Job Training	Employees in these occupations usually need several years of work-related experience, on-the-job training, and/or vocational training.
Job Zone Examples	Many of these occupations involve coordinating, supervising, managing, or training others. Examples include accountants, sales managers, database administrators, teachers, chemists, art directors, and cost estimators.
SVP Range	(7.0 to < 8.0)
	Job Zone Five: Extensive preparation needed
Education	Most of these occupations require graduate school. For example, they may require a master's degree, and some require a Ph.D., M.D., or J.D. (law degree).
Related Experience	Extensive skill, knowledge, and experience are needed for these occupations. Many require more than five years of experience. For example, surgeons must complete four years of college and an additional five to seven years of specialized medical training to be able to do their job.
Job Training	Employees may need some on-the-job training, but most of these occupations assume that the person will already have the required skills, knowledge, work-related experience, and/or training.
Job Zone Examples	These occupations often involve coordinating, training, supervising, or managing the activities of others to accomplish goals. Very advanced communication and organizational skills are required. Examples include librarians, lawyers, sports medicine physicians, wildlife biologists, school psychologists, surgeons, treasurers, and controllers.
SVP Range	(8.0 and above)

component of Worker Characteristics information found in the Dictionary of Occupational Titles (U.S. Department of Labor, 1991). Specific Vocational Preparation, as defined in Appendix C of the Dictionary of Occupational Titles, is the amount of lapsed time required by a typical worker to learn the techniques, acquire the information, and develop the facility needed for average performance in a specific job-worker situation.

This training may be acquired in a school, work, military, institutional, or vocational environment. It does not include the orientation time required of a fully qualified worker to become accustomed to the special conditions of any new job. Specific vocational training includes: vocational education, apprenticeship training, in-plant training, on-the-job training, and essential experience in other jobs.

Specific vocational training includes training given in any of the following circumstances:

1. Vocational education (high school, commercial or shop training, technical school, art school, and that part of college training which is organized around a specific vocational objective)
2. Apprenticeship training (for apprentice jobs only)
3. In-plant training (organized classroom study provided by an employer)
4. On-the-job training (serving as learner or trainee on the job under the instruction of a qualified worker)
5. Essential experience in other jobs (serving in less responsible jobs, which lead to the higher-grade job, or serving in other jobs which qualify).

The following is an explanation of the various levels of specific vocational preparation:

Level Time

1. Short demonstration only
2. Anything beyond short demonstration up to and including 1 month
3. Over 1 month up to and including 3 months
4. Over 3 months up to and including 6 months
5. Over 6 months up to and including 1 year
6. Over 1 year up to and including 2 years
7. Over 2 years up to and including 4 years
8. Over 4 years up to and including 10 years
9. Over 10 years

Note: The levels of this scale are mutually exclusive and do not overlap.

Verifying competency statements. The last pages of your competency portfolio are the verification letters/certificates. Two verification letters are required for work life portfolios (i.e., letters from a previous supervisor, director, vice president, owner, and/ or co-worker). Texas State—OWLS must verify your position and experience for which you are applying for work life. See example verification letter below. Non-collegiate college competency portfolios must also be verified. See the Selecting and Verifying Non-collegiate Training section.

Additional evidence for competency portfolios may include:

1.   Product, such as, work samples, test scores, books, articles, and performance reports;
2.   Certifications, license, rank, grade

Work Verification Letter

Applicant's Name _____   ID _____

Job Title _____

Length of Employment _____ No. of Hours Worked Per Week_____

To be completed by student:
Describe the particular duties you were required to perform in your setting.

What promotions or recognition did you receive?

To be completed by supervisors:
How would you rate the applicant's motivation level? Circle and **initial** the appropriate numeral.

1	2	3	4	5
(Low)				(High)

How would you rate the applicant's interpersonal skills? Circle and **initial** the appropriate numeral.

1	2	3	4	5
(Low)				(High)

How would you rate the applicant's job performance in relation to others in your employment? Circle and **initial** the appropriate numeral.

1	2	3	4	5
(Low)				(High)

Rate the level of management the applicant is required to perform. Circle and **initial** the appropriate numeral.

1	2	3	4	5
(Low)				(High)

Information furnished by _____
                                      Printed Name   Signature   Date

Position _____

Title of Organization _____

Address _____

FIGURE 2.8.   Work Verification Letter.

1. If you are **self-employed** you may present your IRS schedule C form 1040 instead of work verification letters. Make sure your schedule C includes the time period identified on the application for work life experience; in other words make sure that it is for the same period of time.

2. If you are **military veteran submitting for military time** for a military occupation, make sure you submit your last DD 214 and at least one efficiency report that covers the time period identified on your application. The alumnus quoted below in Figure 2.9 describes how he saved by receiving credit for his military service.

Request Your Military Service Records. You may request your military services records online, by mail or by fax. These links will help you start the process.

- http://www.archives.gov/veterans/military-service-records/index.html
- http://www.archives.gov/st-louis/military-personnel/vso/official_military_personnel_file_contents.html
- http://www.archives.gov/st-louis/military-personnel/vso/official_military_personnel_file_contents.html

Selecting and Verifying Non-collegiate Training. Non-collegiate training may also be evaluated for credit if equivalent to college level learning. The competency statement developed for non-collegiate training follows the same competency statement model as that of the work life statements. Student can earn up to 30 hours of credit for non-collegiate training.

- Must develop a job task analysis for your training
- Must be at college level learning
- Must be able to verify
- Date of completion
- Location completed
- Number of contact hours
- Must have a course syllabus

As a Veteran it's tough to find a program that lets you maximize credit taken at other colleges and gives credit for military service. The BAAS degree delivers on both. It easily shaved a year off of my degree.

- Dan Reif, BAAS

FIGURE 2.1. Testimonial of Dan Reif

- Must write eight competency statement per 40 contact hours (maximum credit award is 30 hours).

The American Council on Education's (ACE) College Credit Recommendation Service (CREDIT) connects workplace learning with colleges and universities by helping adults gain access to academic credit for formal courses and examinations taken outside the traditional classroom. Find your course or exam at http://www2.acenet.edu/credit/?fuseaction=search.main. If your training or course is recognized by ACE CREDIT, make sure to list the course number on the Non-Collegiate Application.

SUMMARY

PLA validates college level learning outside of a college or university. CAEL advocates assessment can be more than just a tool for measuring learning. It is also a tool that, when done well, can help the learning process. Your competency portfolio is the manuscript that documents your skills, knowledge/cognitive processes, and tools and technology acquired from working and/or non-collegiate training. Each portfolio is assessed for college-level learning by two independent assessors. The two assessors' ratings are averaged and correlated with the academic credit recommendation. Please do not be misled by the 1-hour credit designation for OCED 4111 Prior Learning Assessment. Actually, you are providing documentation for up to a maximum of 24 hour work life credit award and/or a maximum of 30 hour non-collegiate credit award, by doing so saving thousands of dollars and accelerating your graduation timeline.

Upon completing OCED 4111 Prior Learning Assessment, you will develop and submit a competency portfolio that includes:

Page 1.	Work Application (typed and notarized)
Page 2.	Position Description
Page 3.	Job Task Analysis
Page 4.	Competency Statements begin. Each competency statement should be 1–2 pages maximum. Remember that a life work portfolio requires a minimum of 8 competency statements with up to 25 competency statements for a potential 24 hour credit award. A non-collegiate sponsored learning portfolio requires a minimum of 8 competency statements with up to 32 competency statements for a potential 30 hour competency award. .

The final pages of your competency portfolio are the verification letters, certification, and other evidence supporting your work life and/or non-collegiate sponsored instruction application(s). The completed PLA competency portfolio should be saved as a pdf file and uploaded to TRACS as directed by the OCED 4111 instructor.

REFERENCES

Anderson, L. W., & Krathwohl, D. R. (Eds.) (2001). *A taxonomy for learning, teaching, and assessing: A revision of Bloom's Taxonomy of educational objectives.* Boston, MA: Allyn & Bacon.

Heer, R. (2012). *Model of revised Bloom Taxonomy.* Iowa State University Center for Excellence in Learning and Teaching. Retrieved from http://www.celt.iastate.edu/wp-content/uploads/2015/09/RevisedBloomsHandout-1.pdf

Krathwohl, D. R. (2002). A revision of Bloom's Taxonomy: An overview. *Theory into Practice, 41*(4), 212–218. Retrieved from http://www.depauw.edu/files/resources/krathwohl.pdf

O*Net Online. (2017). *Build your future with O*Net Online* [Data file]. Retrieved from https://www.onetonline.org/

Pierson, M. J. (2002). *Discovering your hidden degree.* Peosta, IA: Eddie Bowers Publishing.

Younger, D., & Marienau, C. (2017). *Assessing learning: Quality standards and institutional commitments* (3d ed.). Chicago, IL: Kendall Hunt Publishing.

CHAPTER 3

USEFUL RESOURCES FOR ALL COURSES

"The OWLS program actually gave me a new chance at life...critical thinking, great communication skills, being a good writer, [and] the ability to work with people... are the things that I learned from the OWLS program."

- Michael Guzman, M. Ed.

FIGURE 3.1.   Testimonial from Michael Guzman.

This chapter includes a set of resources we think you'll find useful in all your Texas State University courses. They may also be supplemented by links to other Internet resources, some from Texas State and others that link to resources from a wide variety of other organizations. These are some of the resources that creates exceptional learning experiences such as the one described by the alumnus in Fig. 3.1 possible.

SECTION ONE:
WRITING RESOURCES

For many people, the thought of "formal" or academic writing is disquieting, anxiety provoking and may conjure sensations such as sweaty palms and a racing heart rate. Some may not experience these symptoms but may procrastinate, worry about what to write about, or get stuck while figuring out where to start. The good news is, there are time-proven ways to address these issues. Another piece of good news is, you probably already spend more time writing than you think.

In your everyday life, several times a day you compose email messages, Facebook posts, Instagram captions, tweets, texts, etc. You probably also fill out forms, create lists, and take notes. These, too, are forms of writing. For each venue in which you write, different rules apply. For example, if you are sending an email message to your supervisor, chances are you will use formal language and complete sentences. If you are confirming plans with a friend via text message, you may use nonstandard spellings or "textese" such as "cu2nite @ Marty's." If you are sending a tweet, you may customize it with a really great headline in order to pack your message into 140 characters and to get as much traction on social media as possible. These kinds of writing were probably initially difficult for you and now are second nature.

Academic writing, too, can become easy for you. Before you give in to anxiety or dread, keep in mind that academic writing is just another writing venue among those in which, each day, you are already writing—a lot. Academic writing uses many of the same linguistic skills as these other forms of writing. It also comes with its own distinct rules, norms, and conventions that are fairly easy to master. Some major points to keep in mind:

- Academic writing usually, but not always, comes from a recognizable discipline or discourse community. What do we mean by a "discipline" or "discourse community"? History, music, psychology, math, biology, medicine, or engineering are examples of what are called disciplines at a university. People who teach, study, and work in these fields make up that discourse community. In these different academic disciplines or communities, there may be slightly different rules for effective writing.

- Each discipline or community has its own rules regarding how to construct arguments, what vocabulary and language is acceptable, and how to cite sources to build an argument. You may see assignments require a specific "style" of academic writing with acronyms such as AP (Associated Press), APA (American Psychological Association), or MLA (Modern Language Association). For each documentation style, such as those listed here or others, such as Chicago or Turabian, there are instructional manuals available as well as many free resources on websites.
- Academic writing has an identifiable structure. This structure includes Higher Order Concerns (HOCs) and Lower Order Concerns (LOCs).

HIGHER ORDER CONCERNS (HOCS) AND LOWER ORDER CONCERNS (LOCS)

Thinking about writing in terms of higher-order concerns (HOCs) and lower-order concerns (LOCs) is a way to prioritize the most important parts of your writing (Reigstad & McAndrew, 1984) so that you can give the most vital elements the most attention. HOCs are the "big ideas," elements to ensure that your ideas are understood by the reader. HOCs include: ideas and content, audience and purpose, organization and development, and voice. After you have focused on these elements, then you can work with the LOCs, which include word choice, sentence fluency, and writing conventions.

In some instances, HOCs and LOCs may overlap (Severino, 2013), such as when a sentence is so marred with errors that it needs to be revised in order to be comprehensible. In this instance, HOCs and LOCs would need to be addressed simultaneously. Generally speaking, it is best to focus on only one of these at a time (HOCs) and then move on to LOCs so your revision process will be more extensive and efficient.

HOCS

Ideas and Content

- Most assignments will ask you to identify a position, argument or main theme expressed in a clear, understandable thesis statement.
- You will use supporting details (often academic articles and books) to set the context for the thesis, integrate previous thinking on the topic with your new, synthesized ideas, and to offer support of the position.

Organization

- You will organize the ideas in your paper in a logical, organized, and creative manner.
- Your paper will include a formal introduction and conclusion.

- Voice
- You will consider your audience, and use an appropriate voice in your writing.
- The voice in your piece is what will allow the personality of the writer behind the words to "come through."
- The voice of your piece is your personal style.
- Often, in academic writing, the tone will be objective.
- Voice vs. Tone: The voice of your paper is the personal style and the tone is the mood. Another way to think about it is voice conveys your personality and authority while the tone communicates your emotions or attitude.

LOCS

Word Choice

- You will use words that connect with the audience.
- The words you choose will be carefully chosen, strong, descriptive, and energizing.
- Sentence Fluency
- Your sentences will be varied and well-crafted.

	Exemplary	Strong	Proficient	Developing	Emerging	Beginning
Higher Order Concerns (HOCs)						
Ideas & Content *main theme *supporting details	Exception-ally clear, focused, engaging with relevant, strong supporting detail	Clear, focused, interesting ideas with appropriate detail	Evident main idea with some support which may be general or limited	Main idea may be cloudy because supporting detail is too general or even off-topic	Purpose and main idea may be unclear and cluttered by irrelevant detail	Lacks central idea; development is minimal or non-existent
Organization *structure *introduction *conclusion	Effectively organized in logical and creative manner; Creative and engaging intro and conclusion	Strong order and structure; Inviting intro and satisfying closure	Organization is appropriate, but conventional; Attempt at introduction and conclusion	Attempts at organization; may be a "list" of events; Beginning and ending not developed	Lack of structure; disorganized and hard to follow; Missing or weak intro and conclusion	Lack of coherence; confusing; No identifiable introduction or conclusion

(continues)

FIGURE 3.2.   HOCs & LOCs Rubric.

	Exemplary	Strong	Proficient	Developing	Emerging	Beginning
Higher Order Concerns (HOCs)						
Voice *personality *sense of audience	Expressive, engaging, sincere; Strong sense of audience; Shows emotion: humor, honesty, suspense or life	Appropriate to audience and purpose; Writer behind the words comes through	Evident commitment to topic; Inconsistent or dull personality	Voice may be inappropriate or non-existent; Writing may seem mechanical	Writing tends to be flat or stiff; Little or no hint of writer behind words	Writing is lifeless; No hint of the writer
Lower Order Concerns (LOCs)						
Word Choice *imagery *effective-ness *precision	Precise, carefully chosen; Strong, fresh, vivid images	Descriptive, broad range of words; Word choice energizes writing	Language is functional and appropriate; Descriptions may be overdone at times	Words may be correct but mundane; No attempt at deliberate choice	Monotonous, often repetitious, sometimes inappropriate	Limited range of words; Some vocabulary misused
Sentence Fluency *rhythm, flow *variety	High degree of craftsman-ship; Effective variation in sentence patterns	Easy flow and rhythm; Good variety in length and structure	Generally in control; Lack variety in length and structure	Some awkward constructions; Many similar patterns and beginnings	Often choppy; Monotonous sentence patterns; Frequent run-on sentences	Difficult to follow or read aloud; Disjointed, confusing, rambling
Conventions *spelling, caps, punctuation, grammar	Exception-ally strong control of standard conventions of writing	Strong control of conventions; errors are few and minor	Control of most writing conventions; occasional errors with high risks	Limited control of conventions; frequent errors do not interfere with understanding	Frequent significant errors may impede readability	Numerous errors distract the reader and make the text difficult to read

FIGURE 3.2.   Continued

- Your sentences will flow easily.
- Conventions
- Check your paper for spelling, capitalization, punctuation, grammar, and spelling errors.

The HOCs and LOCs rubric (Figure 3.2) below is a way for you and your in-structors to assess the quality of your writing. You may learn more about what instructors are expecting to see in college-level writing by looking at the descriptors for these HOCs and LOCs in the rubric. The use of such a rubric by instructors in OWLS courses provides clearer and more uniform feedback to the student as well as an equitable way to assign points in the process of assessing writing.

WRITING IN THE BAAS PROGRAM

Nine hours of designated "writing intensive" (WI) courses must be completed at Texas State to satisfy degree requirements. In the BAAS program, there are several classes that are coded as writing intensive (WI). In order for an undergraduate course to be designated as writing intensive, at least 65% of the course grade must be based on written exams or assignments, and at least one assignment must be 500 words or more length. In the BAAS degree, writing is used as a method to improve and measure critical thinking. In the critical thinking section of this chapter, there are excellent resources that you can use to shape and construct your written assignments for this program.

APA STYLE

In OWLS classes in the BAAS program, you will use the APA writing style (commonly referred to as APA). Using APA supports two important writing objectives—clearly communicating content and avoiding plagiarism of others' ideas. First, following APA writing guidelines removes "noise" for readers, so they can focus on your paper's content. This is accomplished in a variety of ways: standardized format and organization, writing clearly and concisely, and using writing conventions such as good spelling, capitalization, punctuation, and grammar (see Lower Order Concerns (LOCS) above; (Reigstad, & McAndrew, 1984)). You may want to create an APA-formatted template in Word addressing APA's most common formatting guidelines:

- 8-1/2 × 11-inch paper with 1-inch margins
- Times New Roman, 12-font
- Double-spaced with no extra line or space before or after headings or paragraphs
- New paragraphs indented five spaces—use Word's paragraph box to format or the tab key
- Title page—running head with page number, title, author name, and institution
- Header with page number (after title page)
- Headings for major sections and, if a lengthy paper, within sections

A formatted and organized paper with a descriptive title, logical headings, good grammar, accurate punctuation, and no typos will clearly communicate your content to the reader. Second, following APA citing and referencing guidelines will help you avoid plagiarism. Strictly prohibited, Texas State University's *The*

Honor Code website (n.d.) defines *plagiarism* as "the appropriation of another's work and the inadequately or inappropriately acknowledged incorporation of that work in one's own written, oral, visual or the performance of an original act or routine that is offered for credit" (Violating the Honor Code, para. 13). In higher education, we frequently use others' ideas our writing! For example, in a research paper, you might summarize others' ideas in your own words, known as paraphrasing, and sparingly quote the experts word-for-word. In both cases, APA requires you to cite the source in the paper's body or text and provide a corresponding reference at the end of the paper.

At this point, you may be asking a variety of questions: How do I structure an APA paper? What format do I use? When do I use a semicolon versus a comma? What words do I capitalize? How do I cite and reference? The authoritative guide for APA is the 6th edition of the *Publication Manual of the American Psychological Association* (Dugan, 2009). In addition, the official APA Style website provides free resources, including frequently asked questions, an APA style blog, and quick answers for references and formatting. You can even follow APA on Twitter, Facebook, and Google+! Other free resources include the Purdue Online Writing Lab (OWL) (Purdue Online Wriitng Lab, 2015) (select APA not MLA), John Dugan's (2009) *APA 6th Edition: An Overview of the Basics*, and Texas State University Writing Center (n.d.) workshops. Texas State's Albert B. Alkek Library (n.d.) provides access to citation management tools, such as EndNotes and RefWorks, to help you manage, cite, and reference resources.

Lastly, don't let APA or perfection impact your writing productivity! When you write, just write. (That's why it's called a draft.) Get your ideas out on paper; generate as much content as you can. Later, in a separate session, return to your paper and edit for format, organization, clarity, conciseness, spelling, capitalization, punctuation, and grammar. You don't want to spend time editing writing that doesn't make it to the final draft. In summary, use HOCs, LOCs, and APA to guide your writing, so you efficiently and effectively share your ideas and content with others in your writing.

REFERENCES

American Psychological Association. (2009). *Publication manual of the American Psychological Association* (6th ed.). Washington, DC: Author.

Dugan, J. (2009). *APA 6th edition: An overview of the basics*. Retrieved from http://www.valdosta.edu/colleges/education/curriculum-leadership-and-technology/documents/APA6thEditionGuide.pdf

Purdue Online Writing Lab. (2015). *APA style*. Retrieved from https://owl.english.purdue.edu/owl/section/2/10/

Reigstad, T. J., & McAndrew, D. A. (1984). *Training tutors for writing conferences*. Urbana, IL: National Council of Teachers of English.

Severino, C. (2013). *Error gravity, HOCs, and LOCs*. Panel at the Midwest Writing Centers Association Conference, Skokie, IL.

Texas State Albert B. Alkek Library. (n.d.). *Citation management tools: Home*. Retrieved from http://guides.library.txstate.edu/c.php?g=450962&p=3079005

Texas State University. (n.d.). *The honor code*. Retrieved from http://www.txstate.edu/honorcodecouncil/

Texas State University. (n.d.). *Writing center*. Retrieved from http://www.writingcenter.txstate.edu/

SECTION TWO: RESOURCES FOR RESEARCH IN THE BAAS DEGREE. WHAT DO WE MEAN BY "RESEARCH" IN THE UNIVERSITY?

You may have heard the word *research* bantered about in discussions at work or the university or with people who are university students or faculty. In a general sense, research is applied to any sort of fact-finding or truth-finding endeavor. For example, you might hear someone say, "I need to research the cost of housing in San Marcos" or "Let's research how to plan our wedding." These are general ways of using the word research, but at universities we use the word more specifically. We want to introduce you to two uses of the term for academics and then share what you need to know about research for succeeding in your degree. A research paper for a course is an example of the first use. You may be expected to do a *research paper* as an assignment. Although this is not a very specific term, in our experience, research papers often require students to find and review articles and other scholarly materials from an academic library or other academic sources, to do one of several things:

1. Support an idea or argument using academic and professional sources
2. Synthesize two disparate ideas or concepts
3. Describe and theorize about some concept or process or event
4. Describe how academic sources might be applied to situations in a profession
5. Evaluate recent findings published in academic or professional sources

In this first use of the term related to writing a research paper, you'll be expected to identify and review academic or professional research articles found in peer-reviewed journals.

The second use of *research* is a more specific term that describes a process of systematic and disciplined inquiry to answer a question or prove a hypothesis. Research in the natural and social sciences uses empirical evidence (primary quantitative or qualitative evidence based on observation or experimentation). In this more specific use, research with empirical evidence is designed to produce some new knowledge. Some research processes may use non-empirical evidence, not based on sources of observation but derived from meta-reviews of literature, analysis of secondary data, theory-building, analytical modeling, futurism and scenario building (Clarke, 2003).

WHAT TYPES OF PUBLICATIONS ARE USEFUL FOR YOUR RESEARCH?

It will be helpful to describe and define the sorts of writing you might encounter as a student in the BAAS degree program. First you may, at times, read what is termed *popular press* publications. These publications are written for wide-ranging public audiences. Publications in this category include newspapers, most newsletters, many trade books that are available at "non-academic" bookstores, and most magazines. Even things like cookbooks, manuals for consumer goods, and many news websites are included here. Some characteristics of this category include use of language that generally does not require an academic degree or technical expertise to read and understand. These materials are usually distributed in large numbers via general bookstores, drug stores, and discount stores. These materials may be written by academic authors, but the audience in mind is a general public (non-academic) audience.

A second category of written material for a specific discourse community requires a more technical vocabulary and knowledge to understand, meaning they are not necessarily accessible to the general public audience described in the previous category. Both trade publications, written for members of a certain occupation, such as retail managers, computer technicians, or farmers, or technical documentation are included in this category. These books and journals are for professionals with a deep understanding of a particular discipline. Technical documentation might include technical instruction manuals, procedural documents, or legal documents. This category typically assumes you do not need to have every term defined or need to be told about the basic theories and practices referred to in the articles.

A third category, and the one that will be discussed in more detail here, is called scholarly or academic materials. This category includes a variety of materials, such as journal articles, academic books, and research reports. These materials are written by authors who are generally professors in the arts, social and physical sciences, engineers, or advanced graduate students, and are intended for an academic audience with advanced degrees in academic disciplines and professional fields. These materials are written with the assumption of previous knowledge of the field, and, in general, do discuss both the theoretical and practical aspects of a topic. Usually, the writing includes documentation about the sources of concepts, theories, and how research results were derived. Academic materials generally discuss the methods of producing the findings openly, so that they may be subjected to scrutiny by those who are pursuing similar research. Your faculty members with the titles of Assistant Professor, Associate Professor, and Professor, who are either tenured or are tenure eligible, are required to produce this kind of scholarship, which may include writing academic materials used in BAAS courses.

Although not all faculty members are expected to produce this sort of scholarship, many also contribute to a wide variety of academic publications. Also, not all universities have this research and publication expectation. Those universities that have research as a mission generally include this requirement, which includes Texas State University. Some writing at this level is purely theoretical, while other writing at this level does include some component of guiding practice or application within a field. It may describe, for example, how a new teaching intervention worked in a controlled trial, to increase student test scores. Then, there may be suggestions about what teachers may do to utilize the intervention. It will not, however, just teach teachers about the intervention and suggest how they utilize it in the classroom. (This would fall into the second type of material, trade publication.)

WHAT IS A PEER-REVIEWED ARTICLE?

Some, but not all, materials that are academic in nature are described as peer-reviewed. You may have heard this term discussed or have a requirement to utilize some peer-reviewed materials in your writing assignments. This peer review process can have many variations, but *blind peer review* (described below) in which the reviewers and original authors do not know the identity of each other, is considered the most rigorous academically.

Let's look at an example about how peer review works. In this example, imagine that Professor A and Professor B have collaborated to write a manuscript for submission to an academic journal. (A manuscript is what we call "a paper" in academic terms, before it is published, so it's not an article yet.) Their manuscript is approximately seven thousand words describing a research study they completed. They have written it for the *Journal of Academic Studies (JAS)*. (This is not a real journal as far as we know. Most journals are much more focused.) Professor C, at another university, is the editor of the *JAS*. Professor A is the first author, so she manages the correspondence and the manuscript. First author means she has written more of the paper than the second author. Most likely, she has also managed the writing of the paper too, integrating the second author's work into the manuscript so it reads well.

Professor A goes to the website of *JAS* and uploads the manuscript in a format without any author names on it. She also uploads an information page that contains the title, the names of authors and contact information for authors, etc. Professor C sends an e-mail to Professor A acknowledging that the manuscript has been received. Professor C scans the manuscript and sees that it is within the *scope* of the journal—meaning the topic fits the journal. Professor C also checks to see that it is a complete manuscript and an appropriate length for publication.

Then Professor C looks through the list of reviewers and associate editors (other professors and scientists from around the region or world) with relevant expertise to review the manuscript without knowing who wrote it (i.e. are blind to knowing the authors' names). The reviewers read the manuscript, make comments and a recommendation about whether the manuscript meets the standards of the discipline and is suitable for publication. These recommendations may be to publish as written, accept for publication with pending revisions (meaning minor revisions are needed), request major revisions and further review (sometimes called *revise and resubmit*), or reject. Once *JAS* has agreed to publish the manuscript in the form eventually presented, then several agreements, including permission to print and a copyright agreement are completed. *JAS* finally prints the paper as an article. The article itself may come out a year or more after it has been accepted.

Academic books may or may not utilize peer review. This is not something that is easy to tell just by knowing the publisher or title of the book or chapter within a book. One common type of book, which does have some degree of peer review is an edited book, which means that one or more professors or professional authors manage the book and ask other researchers to submit chapters, which may or may not be peer reviewed for the text.

College textbooks are yet another type of academic book. They may be subject to review, but are not considered original scholarship—rather they typically rely on previously published material and synthesize these materials into a book that makes sense for students. This book you are reading for BAAS courses is a textbook, and while quite relevant for your coursework, should not be regarded as original scholarship in the same way a journal article is the report of original research.

The discussion of research and scholarly publications here is overly simplified, and there are many nuances to the process. Indeed, each academic discipline does scholarship slightly differently and has its own standards. These standards define what counts as truth and how scientists, academics, and other researchers "do" science in order to develop new findings that are rigorous so they will be integrated into the body of knowledge in a given discipline. As you can see, this is an involved process, takes lots of time, and creates personal ties to the sorts of topics that academics research. So, the adage goes, if you want a professor to talk for hours, ask him or her about his research or research projects! Maybe we won't talk for hours, but it is at the core of what we do as faculty members who do research.

SECTION THREE: INTRODUCTION TO CRITICAL THINKING

This overview of critical thinking takes a close look at the definitions, terms and processes of critical thinking. It serves as an introduction to Lesson 2 of CTE 3313E. This overview is divided into three parts. Part I presents some definitions of critical thinking. Part II introduces two essential dimensions of thinking: identifying the elements of effective thinking and standards to assess the quality of critical thinking. Part III presents some examples of critical thinking processes.

PART I—WHAT DO WE MEAN BY CRITICAL THINKING?

The importance of critical thinking has been recognized as necessary in all levels of education for many years. It has often been taught from a philosophical or rhetorical point of view. Since the 1960s it has been conceptualized as a set of thinking skills that is often included in calls for educational reform. You will note that the four definitions presented below have much in common. After you've read these examples, take a few minutes to identify those commonalities.

Definition One

The Wall Street Journal, in a 2014 article presented these short definitions of critical thinking (Korn, 2014):

- "The ability to cross-examine evidence and logical argument. To sift through all the noise."
  -Richard Arum, New York University sociology professor
- "Thinking about your thinking, while you're thinking, in order to improve your thinking."
  -Linda Elder, educational psychologist; president, Foundation for Critical Thinking
- "Do they make use of information that's available in their journey to arrive at a conclusion or decision? How do they make use of that?"
  -Michael Desmarais, global head of recruiting, Goldman Sachs Group"

Definition Two

This definition is from a presentation by Scriven and Paul (2003):

Critical thinking is the intellectually disciplined process of actively and skillfully conceptualizing, applying, analyzing, synthesizing, and/or evaluating information gathered from, or generated by, observation, experience, reflection, reasoning, or communication, as a guide to belief and action. In its exemplary form, it is based on universal intellectual values that transcend subject matter divisions: clarity, accuracy, precision, consistency, relevance, sound evidence, good reasons, depth, breadth, and fairness. (p. 1)

Definition Three

Critical thinking is a term used by educators to describe forms of learning, thought, and analysis that go beyond the memorization and recall of information and facts. In common usage, critical thinking is an umbrella term that may be applied to many different forms of learning acquisition or to a wide variety of thought processes. In its most basic expression, critical thinking occurs when students are analyzing, evaluating, interpreting, or synthesizing information and applying creative thought to form an argument, solve a problem, or reach a conclusion.

Critical thinking entails many kinds of intellectual skills, including the following representative examples:

- Developing well-reasoned, persuasive arguments, and evaluating and responding to counterarguments
- Examining concepts or situations from multiple perspectives, including different cultural perspectives
- Questioning evidence and assumptions to reach novel conclusions
- Devising imaginative ways to solve problems, especially unfamiliar or complex problems
- Formulating and articulating thoughtful, penetrating questions
- Identifying themes or patterns and making abstract connections across subjects. (Critical Thinking, 2013).

Definition Four

This final definition of critical thinking for your consideration is from "What is Critical Thinking" by Lau and Chan.

Critical thinking is the ability to think clearly and rationally. It includes the ability to engage in reflective and independent thinking. Someone with critical thinking skills is able to do the following:

- understand the logical connections between ideas

- identify, construct and evaluate arguments
- detect inconsistencies and common mistakes in reasoning
- solve problems systematically
- identify the relevance and importance of ideas
- reflect on the justification of one's own beliefs and values

— (Lau, & Chan, 2014–2015, Section C01)

According to Lau and Chan, "Critical thinking is not a matter of accumulating information. A person with a good memory and who knows a lot of facts is not necessarily good at critical thinking. A critical thinker is able to deduce consequences from what he knows, and he knows how to make use of information to solve problems, and to seek relevant sources of information to inform himself." You will find an interesting and useful discussion of critical thinking with a many more resources (including YouTube videos) on the Critical Thinking Web at the above URL.

Now that you've read and thought about the definitions in these four examples, what do they have in common? Here are a few commonalities that probably stood out: it's a disciplined process; cross-examining evidence and logical argument is important; questioning, analyzing, evaluating, interpreting, or synthesizing information is emphasized; it's a process that goes beyond the memorization and recall of information and facts to focus on thinking about thinking to improve our own thinking.

Notice that Definitions Three and Four introduce "problem solving" as one aspect of critical thinking. What do you think is the difference, if any, between problem solving and critical thinking? This question may occur to you because these two terms are often used almost as if they are interchangeable. Problem

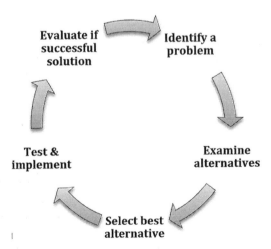

FIGURE 3.3. Diagram of a Typical Problem Solving Cycle.

solving is often presented in the form of steps or, as below, as a cycle with generic steps identified along these lines:

1. Identify the problem;
2. Examine the alternatives (by exploring information and creating ideas);
3. Select the best alternative idea;
4. Implement by building and testing the idea;
5. Evaluate to see if solution worked.

As you can see, this is usually described as a more experimental and mechanistic process with a beginning and an end. This doesn't mean that questioning assumptions and gathering data and information for analysis isn't part of the process—it is. However, the primary focus is on solving a specific problem in a defined timeframe rather than becoming aware of and improving the overall thinking process as we see in critical thinking. In contrast to problem solving, thinking about improving your thinking is a lifelong process!

PART II—ELEMENTS OF CRITICAL THINKING

There are two essential dimensions of thinking we need to understand to develop as fair and open-minded critical thinkers. First, we need to be able to identify the "parts" of thinking and, second, we need to assess our use of these parts of thinking.

These statements, described by Paul and Elder (2008), are the elements (or parts) of fair and open-minded thinking:

1. All reasoning has a purpose.
2. All reasoning is an attempt to figure something out, to settle some question, to solve some problem.
3. All reasoning is based on assumptions.
4. All reasoning is done from some point of view.
5. All reasoning is based on data, information, and evidence.
6. All reasoning is expressed through, and shaped by, concepts and ideas.
7. All reasoning contains inferences by which we draw conclusions and give meaning to data.
8. All reasoning leads somewhere, has implications and consequences.

The second dimension is framed by this question: "What are the appropriate intellectual standards to assess the 'parts' of our thinking?" There are many standards appropriate to the assessment of thinking as it might occur in this or that context, but Paul and Elder (2008) argue that some standards are virtually universal (that is, applicable to all thinking): clarity, precision, accuracy, relevance, depth, breadth, and logic.

How well we reason depends on how well we apply these universal standards to the elements (or parts) of thinking. What follows are some guidelines that are helpful to use as we work toward developing our reasoning abilities (adapted from Paul & Elder, 2008). These are also applicable when thinking through your approach to writing projects.

1. All reasoning has a purpose.
   - Develop a clear statement of your purpose.
   - Choose an important and realistic purpose.
   - Review your thinking (or writing) to be sure you are clearly focused on that purpose.
2. All reasoning is an attempt to figure something out, to settle some question, to solve some problem.
   - Frame the question clearly and accurately.
   - Try framing the question in different ways to clarify and define its scope.
   - Develop sub-questions (if appropriate).
   - Analyze the question to identify if it has one right (factual) answer, is a statement of opinion or needs to be attacked from multiple points of view to develop a complete response.
3. All reasoning is based on assumptions.
   - Clearly identify your assumptions to determine whether they are justifiable and relevant.
   - Consider how these assumptions shape or influence your point of view.
4. All reasoning is done from some point of view.
   - Analyze and identify your point of view.
   - Research to identify other points of view and identify their clarity, precision, accuracy, relevance, depth, breadth, and logic.
   - Try to be fair and open-minded when researching and evaluating all points of view.
5. All reasoning is based on data, information, and evidence.
   - Make sure your statements and claims are supported by the data identified during your research.
   - Research to identify data, information, and evidence that opposes your position as well as supports it.
   - Make sure that all information and evidence is relevant to the question and clearly and accurately stated.
   - Make sure you have sufficient information and evidence to support the arguments for your point of view.
6. All reasoning is expressed through, and shaped by, concepts and ideas.
   - Identify key concepts and discuss them clearly.
   - Consider other concepts and all definitions of key concepts.
   - Describe and use concepts carefully and with precise language.

7. All reasoning contains inferences by which we draw conclusions and give meaning to data.
   * State only inferences that are implied by the evidence.
   * Compare inferences for logical consistency with each other.
   * Identify underlying assumptions leading to your inferences.
8. All reasoning leads somewhere, has implications and consequences.
   * Identify and follow the logical implications and consequences of your reasoning.
   * Include analysis of the negative as well as positive implications.
   * Be open to all possible negative and positive consequences.

PART III—THREE EXAMPLES OF CRITICAL THINKING PROCESSES

This section presents examples of applying to a question or issue the eight elements of the critical thinking process described above by Paul and Elder (2008).

Example One: Applying Critical Thinking to Make a Technology Purchase

You've been saving money to buy a new computer for use at home. The text in *italics* presents some of the ideas and questions that might come to mind as you critically think through making this purchase.

What are some of the assumptions you might have about what you want? You want a bigger monitor, more memory, faster processors, etc., right? Or maybe you want a laptop or a tablet this time? Do I have enough money? This is time to think clearly about the purpose for this computer.

* All reasoning has a purpose.
  So what do I need this computer to be able do?
* All reasoning is an attempt to figure something out, to settle some question, to solve some problem.
  Do I really need a bigger monitor? Is a desktop better at home—or would it help to have a laptop to use at the library or while traveling and take it work? I really like tablets because they are smaller and good for games. I like my Mac Operating System (OS) so I may want to keep using an Apple.
* All reasoning is based on assumptions.
  Wait a minute—is this just for me at home? What about my spouse and the kids? Do I want the kids asking to play games on my tablet all the time? What OS do I need to be able to use it at work? If I want a laptop for work projects and when traveling on business, maybe I need to convince my employer to buy one for me? Then maybe we can buy a tablet—maybe two—for use at home?

- All reasoning is done from some point of view.

    OK—I need to do some research and compare information about desktop computers versus laptops versus tablets. What are the pros and cons, based on the purpose(s) I decided on and what will be the primary uses of this type of computer. And based on how much I can afford to pay? It looks like a Windows OS is less expensive than an Apple OS.

- All reasoning is based on data, information, and evidence.

    Now that I've done my research (by reading reviews, going to stores, talking with the family, an IT person at work, and friends, etc.), what ideas about these various types of computers have I learned that seem to be the best reasons for selecting this type of computer?

- All reasoning is expressed through, and shaped by, concepts and ideas.

    We don't need a bigger monitor and faster desktop because nobody in the family wants to be limited to a desktop at home any more. The new laptop/tablet configuration let's me use the Windows OS at work and a tablet for use at home. My employer is providing "loaner" laptops for special projects and travel so that's no longer a big factor.

- All reasoning contains inferences by which we draw conclusions and give meaning to data.

    Now I'm ready to purchase one of the new laptop/tablet combinations that will provide the Windows OS for work and gives me a tablet for family and personal use as well. We've also decided as a family to buy a new game system for the kids to play on with our recently purchased internet enabled TV. Now—what kind of game system do we need to buy?

- All reasoning leads somewhere, has implications and consequences.

Example Two: Applying Critical Thinking to Career Transition/ Change(s)

This example presents a situation where critical thinking is applied to the question of career transition/change. This is a more complex situation so only the big picture topics and questions are presented in italics. There are many more questions and contingencies an individual would need to address. And since this process probably plays out over some length of years, other life events and contingent decisions will inevitably happen to add complexity.

So, in a quiet moment of reflection you find this question has popped into your consciousness: *What am I doing with my life? How are things going with our family and at work? What's making me tense or anxious? What makes me happy—or not? What makes me happy and feeling fulfilled at work? What do I not like about my work? What might make my life better—happier and more fulfilling?*

- All reasoning has a purpose.

    What might make my life better—happier and more fulfilling? What do I want to do with my life?

- All reasoning is an attempt to figure something out, to settle some question, to solve some problem.

    As you are reading this, you'll have to help fill in the blanks with some critical thinking for this example—even if it is only hypothetical in your situation. *What are some of the assumptions your life was/ is based on? Graduating from high school and getting a good job in _____? Going into the military? Getting married and having children? Living life as a surfer dude or ski instructor? Going to college? Becoming a doctor or lawyer as your parents expected?*

- All reasoning is based on assumptions.

    At this point in my life, at age _____, what can I realistically do? Does my decision affect the lives of others or is it primarily going to impact me? If it affects others, is it reasonable that I ask them to support me through whatever I decide to do?

- All reasoning is done from some point of view.

    Ok—is this just wishful thinking or when I do a "gut check" do I find the motivation and persistence to see this process through to completion? What are my options? Do I need further training to make the next step(s) in my current work to get to _____ (insert level, rank, or job title here)? Do I want to stay in this line of work but get into a different sector? Do I want to change careers entirely and go into _____ (insert ideas here)? To achieve this transition, do I need a community college degree? A four-year college degree? A graduate degree? What information can I find from state and Federal employment services, libraries, internet resources, career counselors, talking with people already employed in this possible new career, etc.?

- All reasoning is based on data, information, and evidence.

    Based on my research, these are the life/work ideas that mean the most to me and seem to describe my best options: _____ _____.

- All reasoning is expressed through, and shaped by, concepts and ideas.

    Wow—this is exciting! I've decided to _____ _____ because it is my best option and leads to changes that will make my life more fulfilling.

    So how do I get started? I know—I'll do some of that project planning that we talk about in courses for the BAAS degree!

- All reasoning contains inferences by which we draw conclusions and give meaning.

Example Three: Applying Critical Thinking to Writing a College Research Paper

There is a discussion of effective writing, research and research papers above. This example builds on that information and provides an overview of critical thinking processes for an academic paper at the college level. This is critical thinking as an exploration of questions you're posing about existing knowledge for issues that are not defined clearly and for which there are no specific and clear-cut answers. Typical topics for these papers may include questions related to social, economic, scientific, technological, political, ethical, or spiritual issues—or some combination all these topics.

Sustainability and sustainable development are recent concepts stimulated by taking a more holistic perspective on the web of many interconnected environmental, economic, technological, social and ethical concerns in the late 20th century. According to Rainey and Araujo (2015),

> Sustainability involves meeting the needs of today without disrupting or harming the social and economic well-being of humankind and the natural environment. Sustainability implies that all human and business activities are carried out at rates equal to or less than the Earth's natural carrying capacity to renew the resources used and to naturally mitigate the waste streams generated. (p. 1)

Now you are intrigued by these holistic perspectives articulated by thinking sustainably and want to explore it more in a research paper. This is an even more complex set of issues to explore so only some of the big picture topics and questions are suggested here in italics.

Sustainability is such a broad set of topics with a wide range of interconnected issues, I really need to identify the reason(s) why it intrigues me and how to define an approach relevant to my personal, work or academic interests.

- All reasoning has a purpose.
  What is the question I most want to explore? Do I want to focus on the social or economic or technological issues? Am I interested in the impact of sustainable development on my personal life, or my kids' future or my

professional life and work with a large corporation? What is the future of my company if or when it tries to act sustainably? How do Subaru and other companies achieve zero landfill manufacturing processes?

- All reasoning is an attempt to figure something out, to settle some question, to solve some problem.

   What are my personal assumptions about the impact of human consumption on the Earth? Have I changed my habits any? Should I consume less and do more to reduce, re-use and recycle at work and at home? As I read the literature on sustainability, do the assumptions have logical coherence when considered from these different sets of concerns and this recently described holistic perspective? What other assumptions are in play here?

- All reasoning is based on assumptions.

   As I approach writing this paper, do I want to write it as a concerned citizen or from my professional perspective on strategic initiatives a business might consider?

- All reasoning is done from some point of view.

   The sustainability literature primarily developed during the last 30 years, so I need to look at recent publications. What should my strategy be to identify the types of literature and sources from all these disciplines that will be most useful?

- All reasoning is based on data, information, and evidence.

   Now that I've gathered all this information and evidence arguing that sustainability is the best way to address this web of interconnected issues, what are the big ideas that relate logically to and support the point of view I've adopted?

- All reasoning is expressed through, and shaped by, concepts and ideas.

   Are my conclusions supported logically by the information and evidence discovered during the research phase? What are the positive and negatives implications and conclusions for business processes, for my family and my community?

- All reasoning contains inferences by which we draw conclusions and give meaning.

REFERENCES

Clarke, R. (2003). *Non empirical research techniques* (PowerPoint slides). Retrieved from: www.rogerclarke.com/Res/51-NonEmp.ppthttp://www.rogerclarke.com/Res/51-NonEmp.ppt

Critical Thinking. (2013). *The glossary of education reform.* Retrieved from: http://edglossary.org/critical-thinking/

Korn, M. (2014, October 21). Bosses seek 'critical thinking,' but what is that? *Wall Street Journal Online.* Retrieved from: http://www.wsj.com/articles/bosses-seek-critical-thinking-but-what-is-that-1413923730

Lau, J., & Chan, J. (2014–2015). *What is Critical Thinking?* Retrieved from: http://philosophy.hku.hk/think/critical/ct.php

Paul, R., & Elder, L. February, 2008. *The analysis & assessment of thinking.* Foundation for Critical Thinking, Online. Retrieved from: https://www.criticalthinking.org/pages/the-analysis-amp-assessment-of-thinking/497https://www.criticalthinking.org/pages/the-analysis-amp-assessment-of-thinking/497

Rainey, D. L., & Araujo, R. J. (2015). *The pursuit of sustainability: Creating business value through strategic leadership, holistic perspectives, and exceptional performance.* Charlotte, NC: Information Age Publishing.

Scriven, M., & Paul, E. (2003). Defining critical thinking. *National Council for Excellence in Critical Thinking Instruction.* Retrieved from: http://www.criticalthinking.org/pages/defining-critical-thinking/410

SECTION FOUR:
CREATING A PROBLEM STATEMENT

The focus of this section, building on the previous section on research, is to help you know the criteria to develop a useful and effective statement of a research question or problem as a key to successful research. It is important to understand the process of shaping a problem statement, whether it is a thesis statement for a research paper or more formal observational or experimental research project.

IDENTIFYING A PROBLEM

So what is the problem? All research begins with the identification of a question or problem statement. A problem well-stated is half-answered. That is, effectively stating the research problem is one of the most important elements of research (Kerlinger, 1986, p. 15). Beginning researchers generally have difficulty in problem selection because of the wide range of possibilities. Problem selection often occurs early in studies when their knowledge is limited. Bearing this in mind, do not lose sight of the goal at hand and continue to focus and delimit the scope of the project until you have effectively defined and stated the problem. Reviewing the literature (i.e. journal articles, books, trade journals, newspapers, professional magazines, etc.) will help provide knowledge that will assist in focusing the problem. What are other researchers saying about similar issues? What are the relevant recommendations for future studies? Keep in mind, the less defined your question or problem, the harder it will be to research.

Questions to ask while developing and evaluating a tentative problem statement (Isaac & Michael, 1995, pp. 36–39):

- Am I genuinely interested in the problem?
- Is the scope of the problem too broad? How can I improve focus to narrow it down?
- Is it directly related to my academic module or course?
- Does my academic coursework provide me with the antecedent knowledge to research and successfully complete this project?
- Will this project facilitate access, increase my experience, and advance my career in the desired industry?

- Do I have the time necessary to study the problem?
- Do I have the necessary funds and support?
- Do I have any strong biases regarding the problem?
- Has the problem already been adequately investigated?
- What does the academic and professional literature say about the problem under consideration?

WHY REVIEW THE LITERATURE?

- Knowledge of related literature enables you to define the frontiers of their field. It is the foundation to examine, extend and refine your problem.
- An understanding of theory in the field enables you to place their problem, question, or hypothesis in perspective.
- A thorough study of related research provides an understanding of which procedures and instruments have proved useful and which are less promising and avoids duplicating a study.
- Provides knowledge to understand and interpret the research.
- Offers a historical review of the major concepts related to proposed activities.

WHAT MAKES A GOOD PROBLEM STATEMENT?

A strong problem statement articulates "a clear connection to relevant literature, data, trends or related information to justify the study, and create a strong argument for the research" (Newman & Covrig, 2013, p. 78). Effective problem statements answer the question "Why does this research need to be conducted?" It should succinctly and precisely state what you will study. Your research proposal will not be properly framed if you fail to clearly identify the problem. The problem statement itself is a succinct statement; however, it is generally supported by several other sentences that help to define and shape your research project. Persuasive arguments, opinions of others researchers, futurists, and professionals might be useful references to support the need for study. What are relevant business, social and/or political trends? Provide concrete illustrations of the problem. Make sure you can still easily identify the single sentence that is the problem statement.

Describing a purpose for your capstone activity is the next step after developing your problem statement. The purpose briefly describes the student's action plan intended to address the problem identified. As you will see in the examples below, the problem statement is followed by a purpose that describes your proposed solution to the problem.

WHY DO I NEED TO KNOW HOW TO WRITE A PROBLEM STATEMENT?

Students in Occupational, Workforce, and Leadership Studies are required to complete OCED 4360 *Cooperative Occupational Education Readiness* and OCED 4361 *capstone in Cooperative Occupational Education.* OCED 4360 *Cooperative Occupational Education Readiness* prepares the student for supervised on-the-job experience in an occupational area. The student will develop a capstone proposal that includes a **statement of the problem, purpose, review of literature, timelines, and an evaluation plan**. Students will execute a contract describing proposed activities and begin a 120 hours capstone project. OCED 4361 is the second half of Cooperative Education, where students continue and complete a minimum of 120 contracted hours on the COOP activity followed by approximately 30 hours to prepare the Final Report. Essentially, the capstone is an educational field activity similar to an internship, jointly sponsored by Texas State University and a public or private sector organization. Therefore, it is important for student to know how to effectively craft a problem statement and frame a purpose statement for their capstone. In addition, some of you will continue on to graduate school where you will be required to conduct professional research projects.

EXAMPLES OF PROBLEM STATEMENTS

Let's take a look at some real examples from capstones in Cooperative Occupational Education from previous OWLS students (the names of the organizations have been disguised). While reading the statements, look for the problem statement and analyze how the statement was supported or not. How would you improve each statement? Think about the relationship of the problem statement to the purpose briefly describing an action plan to address the problem identified. What are you considering for your capstone project?

Example 1—A Medical Diagnostic Company

Statement of the Problem: The proposed cooperative education capstone activity is the result of the need for a Medical Diagnostic Company to develop online training (e-learning) modules for their employees. Currently, most employee training is done in a classroom setting with a paper quiz administered to attendees at the end of the session. By creating e-learning modules, the Medical Diagnostic Company can streamline their training process, allow for better documentation of training activities, and identify future training needs.

Purpose: The cooperative education student intern proposes to identify and implement a software program that can be used to create online training (e-learning) modules for their employees.

Example 2—Desert Conservation NGO (Desert NGO)

Statement of the Problem: The Desert Conservation Nongovernmental Organization (Desert NGO) is a bi-national partnership between United States and Mexico entities, both public and private, in the Mojave Desert, Sonoran Desert, Chihuahuan Desert, and Madrean Archipelago eco-regions. Desert NGO science requires geospatial datasets that span the southwestern United States and northern Mexico, with data at spatial and temporal scales relevant to land management, scientific research, and conservation design efforts. Three priority habitats of focus for the Desert NGO are arid grasslands and shrub land, spring habitats, and stream (riparian) habitats. A land cover map at a landscape scale of 30-meters is required as a foundation for Desert NGO science in these priority habitats. The proposed Cooperative Occupational Education capstone activity is the result of a need for a bi-national, integrated, 30-meter land cover dataset. In order to investigate the resources and processes needed to produce this dataset for the extent of the Desert NGO region, a project has been underway since October 1, 2014 to produce a land cover map for one site in the Desert NGO region near the United States and Mexico border. The Cooperative Occupational Education capstone objectives and procedures are based on the purpose of selecting a pilot site using site selection criteria for vegetation mapping and classification

Purpose: The Cooperative Occupational Education Student capstone proposes to select one pilot site for vegetation mapping and classification that is characterized by the three priority habitats of the Desert NGO.

Example 3—NFP Organization

Statement of the Problem: The proposed Cooperative Occupational Education capstone activity is the result of the Not-for-Profit (NFP) Organization of Austin's need to develop an onboarding and training system for their volunteers. Currently, volunteers are brought on and trained at the NFP Organization at the discretion of the director's needs and time constraints. By creating an onboarding and training module, the NFP Organization of Austin can increase the speed of onboarding volunteers, standardize the training of volunteers, and improve retention of their volunteer base.

Purpose: The Cooperative Occupational Education student intern proposes to identify and implement a video volunteer onboarding and training module for the NFP Organization of Austin to use for their volunteers, with a way to update the videos in the future when necessary.

Example 4—City School District

Statement of the Problem: This City School District has more than 8,500 students served by Special Education spread over 129 campuses. Currently, there is no official position, on any of the campuses, designated to coordinate and schedule annual federally mandated Admission, Review, and Dismissal (ARD) meetings to assess the student's progress and update their goals. The lack of such a position and related training leaves coordination of such meetings up to various individuals at the campus level. This absence of continuity among Special Education Departments in City School District can be improved upon if a procedures training manual were created to assist individuals at the campus level to understand their responsibilities within the department, and to guide them in their efforts to efficiently coordinate and schedule ARD meetings for students served by Special Education, thus maintaining state and federal compliance standards.

Purpose: The Cooperative Occupational Education student proposes to author a procedures training manual that describes, in detail, the methodology necessary for scheduling and coordinating Admission, Review, and Dismissal (ARD) meetings in the City School District. It will describe the necessity of maintaining confidentiality, effective communication with parents and teachers, and dissemination of confidential information. At the campus level, the procedures training manual will also outline methods for determining the necessary members of an ARD Committee, organizing and completing the required meeting forms, scheduling throughout the school year in the most effective manner, and implementation of timelines so that Case Managers can ensure each student's Individualized Education Program (IEP) meets state and federal compliance standards.

REFERENCES

Isaac, S., & Michael, W. B. (1995). *Handbook in research and evaluation: A collection of principles, methods, and strategies useful in the planning, design, and evaluation of studies in education and the behavioral sciences.* San Diego, CA: EdITS.

Kerlinger, F. (1986). *Foundations of behavioral research.* Fort Worth, TX: Harcourt Brace College Publishers.

Newman, I., & Covrig, D. (2013). Writer's Forum—Building consistency between title, problem statement, purpose, & research plans and reports. *New Horizons in Adult Education & Human Resource Development, 25*(1), 70–79.

SECTION FIVE:
RESOURCES FOR PROJECT PLANNING, HUMAN PERFORMANCE PLANNING, AND CAREER DEVELOPMENT

This section of resources you may find useful in all courses. It includes discussions of project planning, human performance planning (sometimes known as human performance improvement or talent management), and career planning. You will find these resources useful in several of the BAAS core courses as well as your own professional activities and your career and personal development. The OCED courses that you may find these resources particularly useful are identified in the description of each of these topics.

PROJECT PLANNING RESOURCES

Project planning relates to the use of strategies and techniques to monitor progress toward completion of objectives that result in attaining a goal. You begin by defining the project's scope, which establishes the magnitude of what you intend to accomplish, followed by the methods for completing the project. You then analyze the objectives to break them down into tasks. Each task consists of a description of the activity, a start date/time, a completion date/time, resources needed and an estimate of the number of hours you will spend to complete the task.

You will use project planning in your capstone course (OCED4360/4361), which students typically take after completing all other required coursework for the BAAS degree. Here, you will identify a capstone project of 120 hours within the context of an experiential learning model (e.g., apprenticeship, clinical experience, fieldwork, internship, or service learning). You will divide the 120 hours into four objectives where the product from the first objective contributes to your completion of the second objective, which contributes to the completion of the third objective, and so on. You will then take each objective and disaggregate them into tasks that include descriptions, start dates/times, completion dates/

times, resources needed and an estimate of the number of hours you will spend to complete the tasks.

To learn more about project planning, please reference the following online resources:

- ASQ—Project Planning and Implementation Tools http://asq.org/learn-about-quality/project-planning-tools/overview/overview.html
- Project Management—Process http://www.businessballs.com/project.htm
- Project Management Toolkit http://www.mindtools.com/pages/main/newMN_PPM.htm
- International Journal of Project Management (Available online, Alkek Library)
- Quick Guide: 12 Steps to Planning a Project https://www.projectmanager.com/blog/12-steps-to-planning-a-project
- Tools and Techniques of Project Management http://www.acornlive.com/demos/pdf/E2_EM_Chapter_7.pdf

HUMAN PERFORMANCE PLANNING RESOURCES

Human performance planning (sometimes known as human performance improvement or talent management) relates to the design, development, and implementation of activities for improving productivity at the individual, organizational, and societal levels. It is a systematic process that includes the identification of successful performance targets and performance issues where a gap is causing performance problems. Human performance planning includes monitoring the effects of the interventions to overcome a performance gap. One way of doing so is to compare actual levels of performance to some desired or target level. The difference between these two levels defines the performance gap that may be used to determine the effectiveness of intervention implementation, and/or indicate the addition or removal of interventions relevant to the performance deficit.

The analysis of performance gaps may result in identifying issues at the individual and/or organizational levels. Analysis is undertaken to discover the causes of a gap and then, by the application of interventions, to address the specific performance deficits. The type of intervention varies depending on the cause(s). If the cause is due to a lack of technical expertise, for example, then training may be the intervention. If the cause is due to lack of proper communication within a unit or other levels of the organization, then adoption of formal written policies that address specific issues may be the solution.

To learn more about human performance planning, please reference the following online resources:

- Human Performance (journal) (Available online, Alkek Library)
- Human Performance Improvement http://theengagementeffect.com/our-toolset/additional-tools/human-performance-improvement

- International Society for Performance Improvement http://www.ispi.org/
- Ohio Safety Congress—Human Performance https://www.bwc.ohio.gov/downloads/blankpdf/congress10/436humanpart2.pdf
- Performance Improvement: Steps, Stages, and Tools http://www.prime2.org/sst/intro.html
- Society for Human Resource Management http://www.shrm.org/templatestools/howtoguides/pages/performanceimprovementplan.aspx
- UC Berkley HR—Performance Expectations http://hrweb.berkeley.edu/guides/managing-hr/managing-successfully/performance-management/planning/expectations

CAREER PLANNING RESOURCES

Career planning consists of activities and actions designed to help you achieve your individual career goals (or perhaps guide others in the process). The activities consist of self-reflection where you explore your interests and abilities and formulate your career goals. You then identify and act on specific tasks that result in the realization of those goals. You will engage in career planning in many of your OWLS courses for the BAAS degree. These courses include CTE 3313E—Introduction to Interdisciplinary Studies for the Bachelor of Applied Arts and Sciences Degree; OCED 4350—Foundations of Career and Prior Learning Assessment, OCED 4111—Independent Study in Occupational Education; and OCED 4360/4361—BAAS Capstone.

An excellent resource is Texas State University's career website: <u>Jobs4Cats</u>. Here, you will find career related handouts and guides, get help with a job search, arrange to meet with a career counselor, and connect with employers seeking to hire Texas State graduates. Universities usually have excellent career resources and services that adult learners often do not use very fully. If you are in a career transition mode, you may found this office very useful!

You can also learn more about career planning at the following online resources:

- About Careers http://careerplanning.about.com/cs/choosingacareer/a/cp_process.htm
- Career Planning and Adult Development Journal (Available online, Alkek Library)
- Career Planning Four-Step Planning Process http://www.careercentre.dtwd.wa.gov.au/careerplanning/Pages/CareerPlanning-4StepPlanningProcess.aspx
- Developing a Strategic Vision for Your Career Plan http://www.quintcareers.com/career_plan.html

- The College Student's Guide to Career Planning http://gato-docs.its.tx-state.edu/career-services/paperhandouts/career-relatedhandouts/Career-Planning/The College Student_s Guide to Career Planning.pdf
- What is Career Planning and Development http://www.job-interview-site.com/what-is-career-planning-and-development.html
- What is Career Planning and Who Needs It http://www.concordiaonline.net/what-is-career-planning-and-who-needs-it/
- http://www.concordiaonline.net/what-is-career-planning-and-who-needs-it/
- http://www.concordiaonline.net/what-is-career-planning-and-who-needs-it/

SECTION SIX:
INTRODUCTION TO THE INTERNET
AND COMPUTER TECHNOLOGY

We are surrounded by digital electronic devices. We carry smartphones and drive vehicles that keep track of when they need service. Even many elementary school students have phones and carry small tablet computers. The electronic world is all around us. As college students, you too have technology and electronics essential to your success. Access to the Internet and options with mobile technology contributed to the flexibility of the MSIS degree as described by one alumnus in Figure 3.4 below.

Technology is usually defined as "the branch of knowledge that deals with the creation and use of technical means and their interrelation with life, society, and the environment, drawing upon such subjects as industrial arts, engineering, applied science, and pure science." (Retrieved from http://dictionary.reference.com /browse/Technology)

Technology is a vital part of your degree journey as a college student. You may have already used this technology to apply for admission to Texas State, take the student orientation, and explore the University website. This chapter provides essential computer skills, programs, and utilities you will need to succeed in your degree journey. The links in this chapter are available as a list in Appendix B.

"Texas State offered the quality education that was the most flexible that I could actually come to an institution to study and to meet my peers and professors and feel like I was going to college and yet had enough technology and enough trend that I could fully experience online resources, online classes, and online collaboration"

- Lou de Virgilio, MSIS

FIGURE 3.4.   Testimonial of Lou de Virgilio

TEXAS STATE UNIVERSITY NETWORKS AND YOU

One of your first tasks as a Texas State student was to set up your NetID and your password. You will be asked to change that password regularly. Your personal information is held by the University on its computers and regular password changes help protect your information as well as the information of all students. It is a measure of trust the University places in you that you will not endanger that information by sharing your access to the University's network with someone who is not a student.

Be sure to create a strong password that you can remember. A good password has a mix of upper and lower case letters, a few numbers, and a symbol or two. Using an actual phrase such as a poem, common saying, or random words is more difficult for a hacker to guess. You will need that NetID and password to access your online course room, research in the library, as well as check your course schedule and grades. It pays to have a password that is strong and one you can remember.

The University has an e-mail system called Bobcat Mail. Your NetID combined with the phrase "@txstate.edu" constitute your e-mail address while you are a student, for example nid01@txstate.edu. E-mail is the main means the Department of Occupational, Workforce, and Leadership Studies has to communicate with you. You can access your e-mail using the Bobcat Mail link on the University's home page. If you are knowledgeable about using e-mail you can forward this address to another account. (For more information see http://www.tr.txstate. edu/itac/student-support.html.)

COMPUTER HARDWARE

All of this assumes you have a good computer and a connection to the Internet. Because of the demands of online courses, you should have the newest and fastest computer you can afford. It does not matter which operating system (OS) you choose, Apple or Windows, the main point is that the system functions properly. The University has agreements with several companies for discounts on computers and computer systems. (For more information see: http://www.tr.txstate.edu/ hardware.html.)

Taking courses online will require you to have an internet connection that is high-speed and has good bandwidth. Bandwidth is a measure of the amount of code or data that can be passed through to your computer by the Internet connection. It is usually expressed in bits per second. The more bits that can flow per second, the faster your information will arrive at your computer. Many providers have internet available along with your television and/or telephone service. You should get the fastest and most generous service your personal budget will allow. If you are limited in your neighborhood to dial-up telephone modem connection, investigate libraries and cafes that have free Wi-Fi where you may be able to work on a high-speed access network. One important caution is needed about free

Wi-Fi connections at cafes, stores, malls, hotels, and airports, etc. If there is no password needed to access these networks, these are probably not secure connections, so they are an invitation to hackers to infect your computer with viruses or steal your personal information. It is a good idea to not access university services, do online shopping with a credit card or access your bank account on these open Wi-Fi hotspots.

Occasionally, an instructor will announce a synchronous (scheduled for a particular date and time) course meeting. In this situation, you need a camera and microphone to be seen and be heard by your fellow students. Many laptop computers come equipped with these built-in, but many desktop systems do not. Again, it depends on your budget. Headsets with earphones and microphones that function well can be purchased without spending much money. Some newer model monitors have cameras built in, or you can purchase a small one to clip on the monitor. These are also essential if you want to produce a narrated presentation for a course project.

BASIC COMPUTER SKILLS

You need to have some basic computer skills to be successful in university courses. If you are like many users, you know just enough to answer your e-mail and post something to social media. There are some excellent tutorials on GCFLearnFree.org to help you learn more about the basic skills you will need. This site includes tutorials on Apple and Windows operating systems as well as many software programs we will be discussing. Here is a list of basic skills and procedures essential to your success:

- Turning your computer on and off
- Opening and closing programs
- Minimize and Maximize dialog windows
- Creating folders, sub-folders, and organizing your files
- Moving files
- Drag and Drop
- Cut and Paste
- Constrained Selections
- Deleting files and emptying the "Trash" folder

ONLINE LEARNING

Your course materials for your courses are posted on TRACS. This is an acronym for Texas State's learning management system (LMS). It stands for Teaching, Research and Collaboration System. An LMS is a computer website that provides utilities for the instructor that enables you to learn the material in a course. It also provides you with your own Workspace where you can store work from various classes. You will access the LMS using a link on the front page of the University web page. You will need to use your NetID and password to enter this secure network. There are some excellent videos available on how to navigate and use TRACS. Each instructor tailors course activities to fit the specific learning outcomes for the course. This means that not all of the utilities in TRACS will be used in every course.

TRACS is supported on desktop and laptop computers using both the Windows and Apple operating systems. You may be successful using other browsers or systems, but these are the ones officially supported. Some portions of TRACS will work on Android (tablets or phones), iOS machines (such as iPads and iPhones), and Linux OS machines, however, not all features may work correctly.

When you work in TRACS, you will often be asked to post something in a discussion area called the Forum. The conversation you have with the other students as well as the answers and comments you post to answer questions the instructor has raised are archived by the University. Each TRACS site is compressed and saved for several years so be professional about what you post. Remember the basics: UPPER CASE IS SHOUTING; never say anything that you would not say in a face-to-face course, and read the other responses before you give your opinion. You will also be expected to give a substantive response in a discussion. This means you should think about what you want to say and make it relevant to the subject at hand. Your instructor may suggest a specific length for a post (perhaps a minimum of 50 or 100 words—or more) to stimulate critical thinking and provide a more informed comment than "I agree" or "I think so too!" which are generally not acceptable. You are expected to contribute your thoughts and perspectives to these discussions.

Social Media

One of the most interesting phenomena of our time is social media. Here we want to talk about the implications and power of social media. They are many different kinds of electronic tools whose nature is so recent that society has not yet completely worked out the dangers or usefulness. First, what do we mean by social media. Google defines it as "Websites and applications that enable users to create and share content or to participate in social networking."

A humorous explanation comes from a t-shirt seen recently [12] :

Social Media Explained

Facebook: I like drinking coffee.

Twitter: I am drinking #coffee.

YouTube: Watch me drink coffee.

Instagram: Artsy coffee photos.

Pinterest: How to make coffee.

LinkedIn: Skills: I can make coffee.

(This shirt is available at http://www.computergear.com/social-media-explained-tshirt.html.)

This list is only a sampling of the most common media venues and their avowed purposes. However, there is another side to social media that must be addressed, the social side.

A new area of expertise has arisen called "digital curation" which is the "…the selection, preservation, maintenance, collection and archiving of digital assets." (Retrieved from http://www.dcc.ac.uk/) One author stresses that everything we post, share, or search for online becomes our online identity because we are the curators of that content. We must be aware that every picture we post on our Facebook page, every search we do on Google, becomes part of an identifiable archive of information in cyberspace. It is saved somewhere and becomes part of who we are in the eyes of the world. All of our course discussions and postings on TRACS are archived by the University and will be saved for an unspecified length of time. Even though we delete something from our own machine, if we have sent a copy to someone else, if we have e-mailed it or stored it in the cloud, it will remain in some form somewhere. It is rare that a digital artifact is totally destroyed. With enough effort, it can be at least partially recovered.

There are sometimes serious consequences when you do something on social media. A recent story on CNN told of a man who filmed himself berating a clerk at a fast food establishment about how he disagreed with the corporate policies of her employer. He was a high-ranking employee of an international company. He posted the video on a social media site. Because he had his name and employer listed on the site, his company was deluged with hate e-mails and he was fired. He has not been able to find work because no one wants to have him associated with their company. While he was entitled to his opinion, posting those opinions for the world to see had consequence.

Another problem that arises in social media is deliberately presenting false information for the purpose of making money. This is accomplished by posting ads with provocative titles termed "click bait" to cause the viewer to click on the ad, go to the web site and read the totally false story. The individual who creates the web site has contracted with a company to post advertisements on their web site and be paid for each visitor. Unfortunately some visitors who have not developed good critical thinking skills, mistake the false stories for true stories and then spread them via other social media platforms. One man interviewed on an international news report admitted he was making a substantial amount of money this way and claimed that there was nothing wrong with what he was doing. He insisted that the viewer should be sufficiently well informed to realize his stories were fictional. This Wikipedia page has a list of some of the fake news pages that it has found: https://en.wikipedia.org/wiki/List_of_fake_news_websites

These new and evolving social media platforms have more force in our society than most of us realize. Social media can be a wonderful way to stay in touch with relatives and friends or it can be a way to ruin the reputation of another or yourself. We all need to take seriously the idea of digital content and be an active curator of our personal files.

SOFTWARE ESSENTIALS

You will need Microsoft Office suite of software (or a similar product) that includes a word processing program, a presentation program, and a spreadsheet for BAAS coursework. There are several available including the free office suite, Open Office. Discounts are available by browsing at the Technology Resources site and viewing software and hardware links. For example, Microsoft Office is available at **no cost** to Texas State students—see the link is provided in the Resources file. You will also need to utilize Adobe Reader or Adobe Acrobat (or another PDF reader) to view PDF files. The Adobe Reader is available free for download from Adobe's website.

Additional resources are available if you are near either the San Marcos campus or the Round Rock campus. Campus computer labs will most likely have the software you need for completing your work, but check ahead. Printing is also available at the campus computer labs. Some of your courses will require other software such as data analysis software, or other programs essential to the content of the course. These will be listed in the course syllabus and many are available from the University at a discount. Check the website listed in the Resources.

SEARCHING FOR INFORMATION
ONLINE AND AT THE LIBRARY

We all know that the internet is huge and growing every day. We hear about how much material is out there "in the cloud" and wonder how in the world we can find anything. Several groups realized this early on and developed tools called search engines to help us find things on the World Wide Web. Search engines work basically by sending small programs out across the Web to scan the words and images found on Web pages. These programs are called *bots*, short for robots, or sometimes *spiders* because they crawl the Web. They return terms from the pages they scan to a database. If you have heard the term Big Data, this is one aspect of that concept—the list of terms and pieces of information found by the search engines. The companies that run these searches, such as Google and Bing, have programs that sort and index the words from the pages into a database. When you write a search, the programs within the search engine will scan the index and find links to pages with the information you are seeking. Some then rank the pages by how many visitors (or hits) that page received. The search engine then gives you a list of pages that its program matched with your search. Some of them may be exactly what you are looking, for but sometimes you look at the list and wonder "How did it get that?" It all depends on how you write the search.

BASIC OPERATIONS FOR WRITING AN INTERNET SEARCH

Search engines use a mathematical system developed by George Boole, a 19th century mathematician. It is referred to as Boolean logic but don't worry, how it is used in the search engine is not as complex as it sounds. You use keywords to describe what you are trying to find. You don't write out full sentences but use special symbols so the search engine can compare what you want to its database. For example, imagine you need information on raising longhorn cattle. If you enter the word longhorns, you will get hundreds of listings for the University of Texas sports teams. Let's look at how you can make the search engine give you what you want.

- The first way is to use the phrase longhorn cattle surrounded by quote marks like this: "longhorn cattle" This will cause the search engine to only return pages with those two words next to each other then pages where both words appear on the page.
- A second way is to use a plus sign instead of the quotes, longhorn+cattle.
- This tells the search engine to find sites that have both the longhorn and cattle next to each other and only those pages.
- A third way is to use a minus sign, longhorns-sports but this will give you sites about things having to do with the University of Texas that don't pertain to raising cattle.
- The best phrase might be longhorn+cattle-sports-University of Texas since UT does not have any agricultural courses.

One symbol can also help narrow down a search. For example, if we were searching for information on UT sports but wanted a particular player such as Earl Campbell. We would write the search like this University+Texas+football | Earl+Campbell. The plus signs ensure we get those words together while the pipe character between football and Earl tells the search engine to filter all the UT football pages and only return the ones with the name Earl Campbell. The plus in his name keeps the search engine from returning any player having Earl or Campbell. Only the names together will be returned. The pipe is the shifted symbol on the backslash (\) key.

Many search engines now have advanced search dialogs that allow you to set up a very complicated search by putting the terms you want to find in windows. The Alkek Library site within the University's website has helpful information on how to design both a simple search and an advanced search. No matter what you are looking for, you may find something about it on the Web. All you have to do is write the search phrase correctly.

CHAPTER 4

OFFICIAL COURSE DESCRIPTIONS FOR OWLS COURSES REQUIRED FOR BAAS DEGREE

This chapter contains the official course descriptions for the OWLS courses for the BAAS degree. Please note that CTE 3313E, OCED 4350, and OCED 4360/4361 are required for the degree. OCED 4111 is not required for all students, depending on several factors. Students should consult with a program academic advisor to see if the prior learning assessment (PLA) process in OCED 4111 is appropriate for their degree completion planning.

CTE 3313E—INTRODUCTION TO INTERDISCIPLINARY STUDIES FOR THE BACHELOR OF APPLIED ARTS AND SCIENCES DEGREE

Course Description

Introduction to an individualized degree and interdisciplinary studies, reflection on past and future career directions, critical thinking, professional communi-

A Guide to College Success for Post-Traditional Students,
pages 85–94.

cation, role of information technology in the workplace, leadership development concepts, writing across disciplines, planning for nontraditional options to earn college credit, including prior learning assessment (PLA), and proposing a capstone experience.

Course Objectives

Upon completion of this course the student will be able to:

- Create a capstone proposal based on their professional and academic experiences, and future career plans.
- Implement the final capstone plan that demonstrates proficiency in applying important learning gleaned from their academic and professional experiences, future career plans, and capstone course assignments.
- Produce a quality online presentation that highlights their capstone plan and experience.
- Demonstrate 21st century workplace competencies in project planning, online technology, and oral/written communication.

Course Overview

The course has 8 lessons:

1. Introduction to University Studies
2. Critical Thinking
3. Introduction to Interdisciplinary Studies
4. College-Level Learning in the Workplace
5. Interdisciplinary Academic Writing
6. Professional Communication
7. Leadership
8. Introduction to the Capstone Experience

How This Course Fits Within the BAAS Degree

This is the entry level course for the BAAS degree and a prerequisite for OCED 4350 Foundations of Career and Prior Learning Assessment. During the fall and spring semesters, it is offered during the 1st 8-weeks, and during the summer, it is offered during the Summer I session and is available as a distance learning class or hybrid class with three live classes. It is normally taken at the beginning of the junior year after the general education core curriculum classes and foreign language (if required) have been completed. It may be used in the professional development module, occupational emphases module, or as an advanced elective depending on the most appropriate placement for an individualized degree plan.

Ethical Considerations

Transfer students may not be aware of the myriad of services available to have a successful academic outcome. Adult students who return to complete a degree after being out of academia for a period of time need updated information on policies and procedures. With the availability of unlimited information on the internet, students need critical thinking skills to discern what is applicable to their goals. Since English is not the first language for some students, there cannot be an assumption that they possess college level writing skills.

Technology Notes for this Course

The course syllabus provides information on hardware and software requirements for the class. In addition, there is information about technology included in the individual lessons. Students will have the opportunity to utilize the services of the Texas State Information Technology Assistance Center (ITAC) for assistance with NetIDs and passwords, BobcatMail e-mail access, virus and malware removal, Microsoft Office, Windows, Adobe software discounts, and additional services. Students at the Round Rock Campus will have access to the Campus Technology Center (CTC) for services such as printing/copying, wireless assistance, software questions, equipment checkout, and technology assistance for computer labs.

Other

Since this will be the first class at Texas State for many students, they need to be informed of the policies for academic advisement and which advisor they will contact for assistance. This will depend on whether they complete coursework on the San Marcos or Round Rock Campus, or as a distance learner.

OCED 4111—INDEPENDENT STUDY IN OCCUPATIONAL EDUCATION

Course Description

This course will provide students advance theory and techniques related to the identification, documentation, and assessment of work life and non-collegiate forms of learning. At the course conclusion, the student will have developed a competency portfolio documenting her/his prior learning to be considered as an instrument for awarding credit. Repeatable for credit with different emphases.

Course Objectives

Upon completion of this course, the student will be able to:

- Identify the components of the O*NET (e.g., Task, tools and technology, knowledge, skills and abilities).
- Use the O*NET to identify job-specific skills, task and knowledge for your occupation.
- Identify the rules and processes for using PLA for credit.
- Select Work-Life Learning for evaluation by identifying the highest job zones in which your jobs functions represent OR Select Non-Collegiate training for evaluation.
- Develop a Task Analysis
- Evaluate example competency statements and distinguish between a 6 point scale where remembering = 0, understanding = 1, applying = 2, analyzing =3, evaluating =4 or creating = 5)
- Write Competency Statements that utilize the elements of a competency statement: Task, tools and technology, knowledge, skills and abilities.

Course Overview

The course has 9 lessons:

1. Introduction
2. Using the O*Net
3. What is Prior Learning Assessment (PLA)?
   a. Multiple Approaches to PLA
   b. Ten Standards for Assessing Learning
   c. How PLA Contributes to Academic Success
4. Job Task Analysis
5. Competency Statements
6. Example Competency
7. How Are Competency Statements Evaluated?
   a. Workforce Learning Performance Indicator Score
   b. Non-collegiate learning Performance Indicator Score
   c. What is a Job Zone?
   d. What is a Specific Vocation Preparation (SVP)?
8. Verifying Experience
9. Eportfolio.tstate.edu

How This Course Fits Within BAAS Degree

OCED 4111 is the bridge to academic credit that is unique to our department. Students may earn up to 54 credit hours via this course, if you have the knowledge and experience. Most students use the credit award to complete the Occupational Emphasis in our degree plan.

Ethical Considerations

We strive to hold ourselves to ethical standards in our everyday lives. Students are encouraged to represent themselves in the most positive light, reflecting their knowledge base, skills, and training. We do not want to exaggerate or intentionally misrepresent knowledge, skills, and competent statements.

Technology Notes for This Course

This course uses Texas State's Learning Management System, TRACS. Students are expected to use TRACS to complete the course, a word processor, and the internet.

OCED 4350—FOUNDATIONS OF CAREER AND PRIOR LEARNING ASSESSMENT

Course Description

Theory and techniques related to the identification, documentation, and assessment of various forms of prior extra-institutional learning. Career and occupational information and reflection on career decision-making are the focus of the course. Students are encouraged to have completed their English core courses prior to enrollment in the course. (This course is Writing Intensive.)

Course Objectives

Upon completion of this course the student will be able to:

- Analyze personal transitions using one or more transitional theories and/or adult developmental perspectives.
- Analyze opportunities for growth related to ways of knowing and personal strengths.
- Describe and categorize prior collegiate learning, learning in the workplace, and non-collegiate learning.
- Develop and Implement a Professional Growth Plan (PGP)

Course Overview

The course has 8 lessons:

1. Introduction to Course and Adult Development
2. Adult Learners in Transition
3. Ways of Knowing
4. Identifying Skills and Job Tasks
5. Reflections on Prior Learning
6. Career Planning and Assessment

7.   Reflection and Defining Future Goals in Education, Career, and Life
8.   Course Completion

How this Course Fits Within the BAAS Degree

This is the second course for the BAAS degree and a prerequisite for OCED 4360/4361. During the fall and spring semesters, it is offered during the 2nd 8-weeks, and during the summer, it is offered during the Summer I session and is available as a distance learning class or hybrid class with three live classes. It is normally taken at the beginning of the junior year after the general education core curriculum classes and foreign language (if required) have been completed. It is a required course in the occupational emphases module.

Ethical Considerations

This course often requires students to "dig deep" into their past experiences, personal strengths and weaknesses, and future dreams. These kinds of reflections can be very personal, disorienting, and possibly unsettling for some classmates. They also take time (and sometimes help from others) to process. Because of this shared experience in the class, it is especially important to offer support to classmates in the learning environment. Think about implementing the "golden rule" and unconditionally accepting all class members, just as they are, in every moment. There are team assignments in this course, and you are expected to contribute and to actively include all team members in group learning.

Technology Notes for this Course

You will need access to a computer with connectivity to the internet for this course. This will allow you to access the TRACS course site. The course syllabus provides information on hardware and software requirements for the class. In addition, there is information about technology included in the individual lessons. Students will have the opportunity to utilize the services of the Texas State Information Technology Assistance Center (ITAC) for assistance with NetIDs and passwords, BobcatMail e-mail access, virus and malware removal, Microsoft Office, Windows, Adobe software discounts, and additional services. Students at the Round Rock Campus will have access to the Campus Technology Center (CTC) for services such as printing/copying, wireless assistance, software questions, equipment checkout, and technology assistance for computer labs.

OCED 4360—COOPERATIVE OCED READINESS <u>AND</u> OCED 4361—CAPSTONE IN COOPERATIVE OCED COURSES

Course Descriptions

OCED 4360—Cooperative Occupational Education Readiness. This course prepares the student for supervised on-the-job experience in an occupational area.

Proposal development, review of literature, creation of timelines, and task analysis are stressed. Limited on-the-job experience begins in the course. (WI)

OCED 4361—capstone in Cooperative Occupational Education. Course is supervised on-the job experience in an occupation related to the BAAS professional development. Requires extensive reports and documentation. Prerequisites include successful completion of OCED 4360. (WI)

Course Objectives

At the end of OCED 4360/4361, students will be able to

- Create a capstone proposal based on their professional and academic experiences, and future career plans.
- Implement the final capstone plan that demonstrates proficiency in applying important learning gleaned from their academic and professional experiences, future career plans, and capstone course assignments.
- Demonstrate 21st century workplace competencies in project planning, online technology, and oral/written communication.

How this Course fits within the BAAS Degree

Completion of the OCED 4360/4361 is required for the BAAS degree, and it should represent the high point or crowning achievement of your undergraduate program. Therefore, you should take great care in identifying an experiential learning experience where you can demonstrate your competencies to others. In so doing, the capstone should launch you into the next chapter of life in both personal and career areas. Yes! There is a post-BAAS life waiting for you. So, why not use the capstone to get you there?

Ethical Considerations

Your capstone contract will bind you, your supervisor, and the instructor-on-record to an agreement specifying what work you will perform to achieve your learning objectives, but also the protocols, procedures, and conditions for all parties to follow toward successful completion of the capstone.

Technology Notes for this Course

This course uses Texas State's Learning Management System, TRACS. Students are expected to use TRACS to complete the course, a word processor, and the internet.

CAPSTONE OVERVIEW

OCED 4360—BAAS Capstone I is the first of a two-course sequence devoted to the development of the student's supervised capstone project sponsored by Texas

State University and a public or private sector organization. In so doing, it provides you with an experiential learning opportunity to apply in a real world setting the theory learned in your Professional Development Modules. Weeks before the course begins, you must submit an application proposing a capstone project to the department's Capstone Coordinator. When your application is approved, you may then proceed to enroll in the course.

Once enrolled, you will engage in completing assignments for department approval to begin the 120-hours of work on the capstone. You should be aware that the course assignments and activities begin one-week prior to the start of the first in-class session. The last assignment of the course is an interim report submitted before you proceed into OCED 4361 BAAS Capstone II. There you will complete the remaining 120-hour capstone and then spend the final few weeks of the course in activities related to site-accountability, final product delivery to the site-supervisor, and report of capstone experiences to your instructor.

Please note: the capstone is a three-party agreement between the student, university, and the site-supervisor. Each party must realize therefore their responsibilities and obligations throughout the duration of the capstone. You will receive further details about the capstone prerequisites at a scheduled capstone orientation in the semester prior to your enrollment in the capstone course sequence. The following graphic organizer illustrates capstone activities per week throughout the two-course sequence.

As shown in the graphic organizer, you will develop and submit to the instructor the following four assignments prior to starting your 120-hour capstone project.

An **Activity Plan** consisting of three sections. The pre-contractual section identifies the activities you completed through the submission of your contract for instructor approval to begin the 120-hours. The contractual section identifies the procedures you will complete resulting in the achievement of an objective, including the start, completion, and estimated hours for each procedure. The post-contractual section completes this assignment and describes activities you will complete through the submission of a final report to the instructor and delivery to your site supervisor of your final capstone product. During this phase, your independent evaluator will also assess each of the products from your four objectives.

An **Evaluation Plan** consisting of your procedures, descriptions of your formative and summative instruments, including a prepared timesheet, Capstone Evaluation form, and four Product Evaluation forms—one for each of the products from your four objectives.

A **Literature Review** of 10 or more narrative pages plus a Reference section. You will begin the literature review with background information and overview of concepts relevant to your capstone project. You will then follow this with two to three additional topics that further highlight your work toward the capstone project based on 10 or more peer-review journal articles, plus information from other sources. Students must follow APA format guidelines for this assignment.

BAAS Capstone
Graphic Organizer

Week	Online Activities	Modules	In-Class Activities
OCED 4360 BAAS Capstone I			
1	View Mini-Lecture Videos (3) Take Online Quizzes (3) Begin drafts for: - Activity Plan - Evaluation Plan - Literature Review	Module 1: Pre-Class Preparation: Capstone Activity Plan, Evaluation Overview, and Literature Review	*Class Does Not Meet*
2	Submit by due date/time: - Activity Plan - Evaluation Overview View Mini-Lecture Video (1) Take Online Quiz (1) Begin draft: Contract Continue Literature Review	Module 2: Intro to BAAS Capstone Course	Review Course Syllabus Fish Bowl Q&A Peer Feedback on Assignments
3	Submit by due date/time: - Literature Review	Module 3: Capstone Literature Review and Contract	Review APA writing guidelines Peer Feedback on Assignments Contract Components Overview
4	Submit by due date/time: - Scanned Contract Signatures - Contract (docx unsigned) Students begin 120-hour capstone per instructor's contract approval - Post weekly blog entries	Module 4: Contract (continued)	*Class Does Not Meet*
5, 6, 7, 8	Students continue to implement 120-hour capstone activities - Post weekly blog entries	Module 5: Capstone Activities	*Class Does Not Meet*
8	View Mini-Lecture Video (1) Submit by due date/time: - Interim Report	Module 6: Interim Report	*Class Does Not Meet*
OCED 4361 BAAS Capstone II			
1, 2, 3, 4, 5, 6	Students continue to implement 120-hour capstone activities - Post weekly blog entries	Module 1: Capstone Activities	*Class meets only in week 1 to review end-of-course requirements*
7, 8	Students obtain signed/dated - timesheet - Capstone Evaluation Form - Product Evaluations (4) Students prepare and submit: - Capstone Storytelling - Electronic evidence	Module 2: Post-Contractual Activities	*Class Does Not Meet*

FIGURE 4.1.   BAAS Capstone Activities

A **Capstone Contract** that serves as a formal agreement between the capstone intern and site supervisor to complete the objectives and procedures, and to follow the rules and regulations of Texas State University per institutional, state, and federal laws. The instructor's signature is required to approve this agreement, and is further signed by the Dean of the College of Applied Arts. Please note: only when the contract is signed by the instructor can a student begin the 120-hour capstone.

At the end of OCED 4360—BAAS Capstone I course, you will also develop and submit an **Interim Report** to the instructor providing an update of your progress in the capstone, including a description of any problems you have encountered and your solutions.

For OCED 4361—BAAS Capstone II, you will submit at the end of the course a storytelling paper where you present your project activities, reflections, and insights from the capstone experience. You will also submit to the instructor an electronic file that contains sufficient evidence of your final capstone product. Your instructor will provide you with guidelines for this submission, in case your site supervisor defines the final product as proprietary.

APPENDIX A

GLOSSARY OF TERMS FOR THE BAAS DEGREE

Disclaimer: These are the most frequently used but not a complete listing of terms you will encounter.

TABLE A.1.

Texas State University	
CATSWEB:	Access transcripts, degree plans, registration
BobcatMail:	Student Email Available through Texas State Website
TRACS:	Online course Learning Management System (LMS)
TPG:	Transfer Planning Guide for another institution
Department of Occupational, Workforce, and Leadership Studies (OWLS)	
BAAS:	Bachelor of Applied Arts and Sciences
MSIS/MAIS:	Master of Science, Master of Arts in Interdisciplinary Studies
MEd:	Master of Education in Management of Technical Education

(continues)

TABLE A.1. Continued.

	Required Classes
CTE 3313E	Introduction to Interdisciplinary Studies for The Bachelor of Applied Arts and Sciences Degree
OCED 4350	Foundations of Career and Prior Learning Assessment. Each student will develop a Professional Growth Plan (PGP)
OCED 4360	Cooperative Occupational Education Readiness (completed last semester)
OCED 4361	Capstone in Cooperative Occupational Education (completed last semester)
OCED 4111	Independent Study in Occupational Education (optional) portfolio development for PLA
	Features of the BAAS
Individualized:	Students select professional development courses and capstone project based on career goals and OE module is different for each student
Interdisciplinary:	Focused on broad general skills applicable to a wide range of occupational opportunities
PLA:	Stands for Prior Learning Assessment. Opportunity to receive college credit for prior learning experiences
Non-collegiate:	Opportunity to receive college credit for documented clock hour training outside of post-secondary education
Testing/Test Out:	Opportunity to receive college credit by testing with CLEP and DSST/DANTE
CPM:	The Certified Public Manager (CPM) certificate can be included in the professional development module
	External Terminology
CAEL:	The Council For Adult and Experiential Learning. Works with accrediting bodies, employers, and education institutions to develop a common language and foundation for assessing prior learning.
ACE:	American Council on Education. Coordinates with colleges and businesses to recognize extra-institutional learning
O*NET:	A free online database of occupational definitions and classifications in the United States. Used when developing a portfolio to be evaluated for PLA.
APA:	American Psychological Association (writing style)
	Degree Audit Report (DAR) and Modules of the BAAS degree
	General Education Core Curriculum (42-43 hours)
	Foreign Language Proficiency (8 hours)
	Occupational Emphasis/Emphases Module (48 hours)
	Professional Development Module (21 hours)
	capstone/OCED 4360/4361 (6 hours)
	Electives (varies)

(continues)

TABLE A.1.   Continued.

Course codes	
ELNA:	Elective, not advanced
ELADV:	Elective, advanced
VE:	Vocational education; coded as non-transferable; BAAS can consider credit
NT:	Non-transferable
WI:	Writing intensive. The majority of the grade will come from demonstrating writing skills. Nine credit hours of WI courses are required for degree completion and will be satisfied by OCED 4350, OCED 4360, OCED 4361
Types of classes	
Live:	Face to face in a classroom with the instructor
Online:	Delivered on TRACS with no live meetings
Hybrid:	
Correspondence:	Self-paced online with no live meetings
Extension:	Offered on or off campus depending on student need, available faculty, and student demand. An example in OWLS is the Certified Public Manager (CPM)

APPENDIX B

LINKS FOR THE INTERNET AND COMPUTER TECHNOLOGY

- These links will help you change your e-mail. (Many of these links must be accessed with your NetID and password.)
  https://tim.txstate.edu/onlinetoolkit/Home/Change-Personal-Email

- This link gives you information on recommended hardware and software as well as access to discounts.
  http://www.tr.txstate.edu/hardware/personal-hardware.html
  http://www.tr.txstate.edu/software.html

- This is the link to Lynda.com, FREE software tutorials paid for by the University.
  http://www.tr.txstate.edu/training/lynda.html

- This is the link for GCFLearn Free. (There are many different tutorials on this site.)
  http://www.gcflearnfree.org/computers/computerbasics

- These are the links for the TRACS help files and information.
  http://tracsfacts.its.txstate.edu

- This is a link for the funny Social Media t-shirt. (It worked in June 2015. It is also available at other sites.)
  http://www.computergear.com/social-media-explained-tshirt.html

- This is the site with some basic information on social media.
  http://socialnetworking.procon.org/

- This is the site on Digital curation
  http://www.dcc.ac.uk/digital-curation/what-digital-curation

- Link to the download of software from Texas State
  http://www.tr.txstate.edu/software/download.html

- Adobe Acrobat Reader download
  https://get.adobe.com/reader/

- Search Directions at the Alkek Library
  http://alkeklibrary.wp.txstate.edu/how-to-look-up-a-specific-periodical[GP13] -i-e-journals-magazines-newspapers/
  http://www.library.txstate.edu/